HIP-HOP STARS

JAY-Z

HIP-HOP STARS

Sean Combs
Eminem
Jay-Z
Queen Latifah
Tupac Shakur

HIP-HOP STARS

JAY-Z

Dennis Abrams

ks°

An imprint of Infobase Publishing

JAY-Z

Checkmark Books
An imprint of Infobase Publishing
132 West 31st Street
New York, NY 10001

Library of Congress Cataloging-in-Publication Data

Abrams, Dennis, 1960-
  Jay-Z / Dennis Abrams.
      p. cm. — (Hip-hop stars)
  Includes bibliographical references and index.
  ISBN 978-0-7910-9551-5 (hardcover)—
  ISBN 978-0-7910-9729-8 (pbk.)
  1. Jay-Z, 1970—Juvenile literature. 2. Rap musicians—United States—Biography—
Juvenile literature. I. Title. II. Series.

  ML3930.J38A3 2007
  782.421649092—dc22   2007020739
  [B]

Checkmark Books are available at special discounts when purchased in bulk quantities for businesses, associations, institutions, or sales promotions. Please call our Special Sales Department in New York at (212) 967–8800 or (800) 322–8755.

You can find Chelsea House on the World Wide Web at http://www.chelseahouse.com

Text design by Erik Lindstrom
Cover design by Ben Peterson

Printed in the United States of America

Bang NMSG 10 9 8 7 6 5 4 3 2 1

This book is printed on acid-free paper.

All links and Web addresses were checked and verified to be correct at the time of publication. Because of the dynamic nature of the Web, some addresses and links may have changed since publication and may no longer be valid.

CONTENTS

Hip-Hop: A Brief History

Like the air we breathe, hip-hop seems to be everywhere. The lifestyle that many thought would be a passing fad has, three decades later, grown to become a permanent part of world culture. Hip-hop artists have become some of today's heroes, replacing the comic book worship of decades past and joining athletes and movie stars as the people kids dream of being. Names like 50 Cent, P. Diddy, Russell Simmons, Jay-Z, Foxy Brown, Snoop Dogg, and Flavor Flav now ring as familiar as Elvis, Babe Ruth, Marilyn Monroe, and Charlie Chaplin.

While the general public knows many of the names, videos, and songs branded by the big companies that make them popular, it's also important to know the holy trinity, the founding fathers of hip-hop: Kool DJ Herc, Grandmaster Flash, and

Afrika Bambaataa. All are deejays who played and presented the records that rappers and dancers delighted themselves upon. Bambaataa single-handedly stopped the gang wars in the 1970s with the themes of peace, unity, love, and having fun.

Hip-hop is simply a term for a form of artistic creativity that was spawned in New York City—more precisely, the Bronx—in the early to mid-1970s. Amidst the urban decay in the areas where black and Hispanic people dwelled, economic, educational, and environmental resources were depleted. Jobs and businesses were all but moved away. Living conditions were of a lower standard than the rest of the city and country. Last but not least, art and sports programs in the schools were the first to be cut for the sake of lowering budgets; thus, music classes teaching the subject's history and techniques were all but lost.

From these ashes, like a phoenix, rose an art form. Through the love of technology and records found in family collections or even those tossed out on the street, the deejay emerged. Different from the ones heard on the radio, these folk were innovating a style that was popular on the island of Jamaica. Two turntables kept the music continuous, with the occasional voice on top of the records. This was the very humble beginning of rap music.

Rap music is actually two distinct words: rap and music. "Rap" is the vocal application that is used on top of the music. On a vocal spectrum, it is between talking and singing and is one of the few alternatives for vocalizing to emerge in the past 50 years. It's important to know that inventors and artists are side by side in the importance of music's development. Let's remember that inventor Thomas A. Edison created the first recording, with "Mary Had a Little Lamb" in 1878, most likely in New Jersey, the same state where the first rap recording—Sugarhill Gang's "Rapper's Delight"—was made more than 100 years later, in 1979.

It's hard to separate the importance of history, science, language arts, and education when discussing music. Because of the social silencing of black people in the United States from slavery in the 1600s to civil rights in the 1960s, much sentiment, dialogue, and soul is wrapped within the cultural expression of music. In eighteenth-century New Orleans, slaves gathered on Sundays in Congo Square to socialize and play music. Within this captivity many dialects, customs, and styles combined with instrumentation, vocals, and rhythm to form a musical signal or code of preservation. These are the foundations of jazz and the blues. Likewise, it's impossible to separate hip-hop and rap music from the creativity of the past. Look within the expression and words of black music and you'll get a reflection of history itself. The four creative elements of hip-hop—emceeing (the art of vocalization); deejaying (the musician-like manipulation of records); break dancing (the body expression of the music); and graffiti (the drawn graphic expression of the culture)—have been intertwined in the community before and since slavery.

However, just because these expressions were introduced by the black–Hispanic underclass, doesn't mean that others cannot create or appreciate hip-hop. Hip-hop is a cultural language used best to unite the human family all around the world. To peep the global explosion, one need not search far. Starting just north of the U.S. border, Canadian hip-hop has featured indigenous rappers who are infusing different language and dialect flows into their work, from Alaskan Eskimo to French flowing cats from Montreal and the rest of Quebec's provincial region. Few know that France for many years has been the second largest hip-hop nation, measured not just by high sales numbers, but also by a very political philosophy. Hip-hop has been alive and present since the mid-1980s in Japan and other Asian countries. Australia has been a hotbed in welcoming world rap acts, and it has also created its own vibrant hip-hop scene, with the reminder of its government's takeover of indigenous people reflected in every rapper's flow and rhyme. As a rhythm of the people, the continents of Africa and South America (especially Ghana, Senegal, and South Africa, Brazil, Surinam, and Argentina) have long mixed traditional homage into the new beats and rhyme of this millennium.

Hip-hop has been used to help Brazilian kids learn English when school systems failed to bridge the difficult language gap of Portuguese and patois to American English. It has entertained and enlightened youth, and has engaged political discussion in society, continuing the tradition of the African griots (storytellers) and folk singers.

For the past 25 years, hip-hop has been bought, sold, followed, loved, hated, praised, and blamed. History has shown that other cultural music forms in the United States have been just as misunderstood and held under public scrutiny. The history of the people who originated the art form can be found in the music itself. The timeline of recorded rap music spans more than a quarter century, and that is history in itself.

Presidents, kings, queens, fame, famine, infamy, from the great wall of China to the Berlin wall, food, drugs, cars, hate, and love have been rhymed and scratched. This gives plenty reason for social study. And I don't know what can be more fun than learning the history of something so relevant to young minds and souls, as music.

Saying Good-bye

In the year 2003, rapper Jay-Z was sitting on top of the world. In just eight years in the music industry, he had released nine full-length albums and collaborated on four additional albums, selling more than 30 million records. He had helped to create a business empire based in the high-profile industries of fashion and music. His personal worth was estimated to be more than $300 million. His name was linked romantically with one of the country's most successful and beautiful R & B singers, Beyoncé Knowles. He had started a scholarship fund, had purchased a part of the NBA's New Jersey Nets, had discovered and helped to develop countless platinum-selling recording artists, had started a film production company, and was considered by many to be one of the best, if not *the* best, rapper of all time. What better time, then, to announce his retirement from the recording business? As he put it in the song "Encore" on his "retirement album," *The Black Album*, "Jay's status appears to be at an all-time high / perfect time to say good-bye."

For Jay-Z, it was time for new challenges. As he said in interviews quoted in *Jay-Z . . . and the Roc-A-Fella Records Dynasty*, "If you're not challenging yourself, you might as well be dead. . . . I've had it with the rap game. Time to focus on other things. That's why I'm retiring. . . . Rap is a young man's game, and I thought about that even when I was young—it has to come to an end."

But Jay-Z being Jay-Z, he wasn't going to ride off quietly into the sunset. His retirement would be just as big as anything else in his career. First of all, there was a new CD, *The Black Album*, boasting an all-star roster of producers and cowriters including Kanye West, the Neptunes, Timbaland, Eminem, and Rick Rubin. The album, serving as both a summation and a farewell, sold over 463,000 copies in its first week of release, topping the *Billboard* 200 LP chart.

The album also received extraordinary critical acclaim. As *Vibe* magazine described it, "From beginning to end, *The Black Album* documents a marvelous career. It's monumental because it's a culmination of Jigga's [one of Jay-Z's nicknames] natural thoughtfulness delivered with transcendent skill. . . . If the most definitive part of his legacy will be the end, then *The Black Album* gives you Jay-Z at all his stages. The masterful, lyrical content leaves no question as to how Jay feels he should be remembered."

Rolling Stone magazine joined the chorus, calling Jay-Z, "The dominant figure of the post-Biggie and Tupac era, he spit cool and witty with devastating flows, dropped classic albums, influenced MCs, changed pop culture and built a tall stack of dollars in the process. . . . Jay-Z has come up with one of the better albums of his career. . . . We've witnessed not

Shawn Carter, otherwise known as Jay-Z, is one of the most popular and successful artists in the hip-hop industry. Aside from rapping, Jay-Z serves as the CEO of Def Jam and Roc-A-Fella Records, co-owner of the New Jersey Nets basketball team, and co-founder of the urban clothing line, Rocawear. A self-made man, Jay-Z's perseverance has led to his extraordinary success as a rapper and businessman.

merely a Hall of Fame career but one of the top-shelf greatest of all time. . . ."

The Black Album was just one part of Jay-Z's farewell. On November 25, 2003, Jay-Z took over New York's fabled Madison Square Garden, holding what was billed as his "farewell concert," which would be filmed for later release. It was a historic moment.

It was, in fact, the first time in years that the management of Madison Square Garden had even allowed a hip-hop concert on its stage. In part, this was due to the unsavory reputation such concerts had earned, often plagued by violence and other legal problems. But some also speculate that the Garden management simply felt that hip-hop concerts couldn't pull in a large enough audience to fill the 20,000-plus seat arena.

As it turned out, both concerns were completely unwarranted. When tickets went on sale for the concert, the first hip-hop concert to be held in the Garden in nearly 15 years, tickets sold out in less than five minutes. As Kevin Lyles, president of Warner Music is quoted as saying in the release film of the concert, entitled *Fade to Black*, "I don't know of another artist who could sell out the Garden in a day." And the show itself went off without a hitch.

The lucky attendees saw the best that hip-hop had to offer. Coming out in support of Jay-Z was a veritable galaxy of guest performers, including R. Kelly, Mary J. Blige, Missy Elliott, Ghostface Killah, Foxy Brown, Pharrell Williams, the Roots (who played as his backing band), Beanie Sigel, and to no one's surprise, Jay's longtime girlfriend, Beyoncé Knowles. Special appearances were made by Voletta Wallace, the mother of the late rapper Notorious B.I.G., and Afeni Shakur, the mother of the late rapper Tupac Shakur.

Despite the guest stars, the evening was all about Jay-Z. As CNN correspondent and *Rolling Stone* writer Touré said, "He's still the main attraction. Nobody can blot out the sun that is

Jay-Z." Changing his outfit five times in the course of the concert, he ran through a song list that included not just material from *The Black Album*, but songs from his entire career. That night, in his first appearance at Madison Square Garden, for the two and half hours he performed, he made the world-famous arena his own.

The interesting thing is, because of all the work it took to put the concert together and make it run smoothly, Jay-Z didn't really have time to realize just how huge the concert actually was. As he said in an interview with www.latinoreview.com, "I couldn't feel it at the time. It took for me to watch the movie to really say like 'Wow, that was huge.' Because at the time, like

VIBE MAGAZINE

Founded by legendary musician and record producer Quincy Jones, *Vibe* magazine aims to be "the voice and soul of urban culture." By featuring articles on R & B and hip-hop music artists, actors, and other entertainers, the magazine makes those elements of black urban culture available to readers worldwide.

As it says on the magazine's website, "Through the prism of Urban Music *Vibe* chronicles the celebrities, sounds, fashion, lifestyle, new media and business born from this art form. With an authoritative voice, *Vibe* creates trends as much as it records them. *Vibe* covers music, educates its readers, and gives back to the community. *Vibe* serves as a portal to a growing, young, trend-setting, multicultural audience. By being excellent journalists and innovative marketers, we are champions of urban music and culture."

I said, with such little rehearsal time, I'm focused on what's coming on next. I was just focused on what was going on, the technical aspect of it, the emotional aspect kicked in later when I looked at it. I was like, 'This is crazy.' When I saw the first 15 minutes, that's when I was blown away."

How could he not be blown away? He'd come a long way from the Marcy Houses and the mean streets of the Bedford-Stuyvesant section of Brooklyn. As he said shortly after the Madison Square Garden concert, "This is a journey for a kid from Brooklyn to play the biggest stage in the world. This was much bigger than that. It was inspiration also, because of where I come from and the fact that I couldn't get a deal in the beginning. It just became this thing." As his long-time friend and protégé Memphis Bleek said in the film *Fade to Black*, "I've known Jay all my life. We come from Marcy Projects. We lived off food stamps. . . . It's like going from the bottom to the Promised Land."

"BECAUSE OF WHERE I COME FROM"

It is because of where Jay-Z comes from that his extraordinary success is so unlikely. As he often tells the groups of students he's asked to address, "I came from nothing to owning my own company. It's real and it can happen and it's a long shot. They say when you play with skill, good luck happens."

As Jay-Z knows all too well, it is a long shot. Growing up black and poor in one of New York City's toughest neighborhoods, it takes a lot more than just "playing with skill." It takes drive, determination, and a fierce will to succeed to overcome the obstacles that life put in Jay-Z's path.

Abandoned by his father at an early age, Jay-Z turned to selling drugs as a way to success. When getting a recording contract proved difficult, he and his partners formed their own company, Roc-A-Fella Records, to distribute albums themselves. Even after achieving success as a rapper, he had to contend with the possibility of imprisonment on assault charges,

Following the release of the 2003 *The Black Album*, Jay-Z held a farewell concert at Madison Square Garden on November 25, 2003. The show sold out in mere minutes. With an array of star-studded guest performers and a sold-out 20,000-seat arena, the concert was a culmination of Jay-Z's success as a performer.

legal suits, and feuds with other rappers, as well as personal tragedies. Each of these alone would be enough to stop most people. But through it all, he persevered, only to announce his retirement as a recording artist while standing at the peak of his career.

How did he do it? How did the man who was born Shawn Carter escape the dead-end life of a street hustler to become Jay-Z, hip-hop artist extraordinaire and multimillionaire? How did he create an ever-expanding business empire? What would be his next step? Would he be able to give up the fame and adulation that comes from being a hip-hop star and turn his back forever on the recording studio? Who, in other words, is Jay-Z?

Marcy

"Shawn Carter was born December 4th / Weighing in @ 10 pounds 8 ounces he was the last of / My 4 children, the only one who didn't give me any / Pain when I gave birth to him & that's how I / knew that he was a special child."

—"December 4th," *The Black Album*

Indeed, Shawn Corey Carter, known to the world as Jay-Z, was born on December 4, 1969. The youngest of four children, his mother is Gloria Carter; his father was Adnis Reeves. He has one brother, Eric, who lives in upstate New York, and two sisters, Michelle (known as Mickey) and Andrea (known as Annie). Michelle works for her brother's clothing line, Rocawear, and Andrea is a corrections officer at Riker's Island.

The family grew up in the Marcy Houses, a public-housing project located in the Bedford-Stuyvesant section of Brooklyn in New York City. The project consists of 27 six-story buildings on 28.49 acres, contains 1,705 apartments that house about 4,290 residents, the majority of whom are African American.

The projects and the neighborhood as a whole, especially in the 1970s and 1980s when Shawn was growing up, were poor, crime-ridden, and awash with drugs. Very few people in the projects had either the money or the education necessary to escape living in public housing and improve their lives. To escape the pain and futility of their everyday existence, many residents turned to drugs—marijuana, heroin, and cocaine. But without the money needed to pay for the drugs, many were forced to turn to drug dealing and other crimes in order to maintain their habit.

A worsening downward spiral of drugs and crime continued throughout the '70s and '80s, culminating in the mid-1980s when a new drug—crack cocaine—began hitting the streets. Made by combining cocaine with baking soda, hydrogen hydroxide, and other ingredients, crack is a crystalline substance that is broken up into small chips and smoked, providing the user with a brief but extremely powerful high. Crack is far cheaper than powder cocaine, and it quickly became known as a poor man's drug. Crack also proved to be extremely addictive, which led to a further surge in crime as users, desperate to get their next fix, would do anything necessary to get it. Life in the area, already difficult, got even worse with the addition of crack.

GROWING UP

When Jay-Z remembers growing up in Marcy, he's capable of seeing both the good side and the bad side. As quoted in *Jay-Z . . . and the Roc-A-Fella Records Dynasty*, he describes it as

...a poor neighborhood, but [one where] you learned loyalty and integrity. You learned to respect other people, because it was a minefield. If you disrespect somebody, or act dishonorable, you get hurt. Somebody puts you in your place. So I learned integrity. It's a beautiful place to grow

BEDFORD-STUYVESANT

When people who don't live in New York City think about New York City, there are certain neighborhoods that come to mind. Harlem is one—the Lower East Side, Little Italy, Greenwich Village, and Coney Island are others. But despite (or perhaps because of) its popular reputation for crime and poverty throughout the 1970s and 1980s, Bedford-Stuyvesant is another such neighborhood.

One reason for this is that the neighborhood is frequently portrayed by popular culture in movies, TV, and song. The famous African-American film director Spike Lee has featured the streets and brownstones of the neighborhood in many of his films, including *Do the Right Thing* and *Crooklyn*. Chris Rock's popular TV series, *Everybody Loves Chris*, portrays Rock's life growing up as teenager in Bedford-Stuyvesant in 1983. The area was also featured in Dave Chappelle's documentary *Block Party*, and it is even mentioned in Billy Joel's hit single "You May Be Right," with the lyrics "I was stranded in the combat zone / I walked through Bedford-Stuy alone / even rode my motorcycle in the rain."

Today the neighborhood has experienced a rebirth and is perhaps best known for the sheer number of rap, R & B, and hip-hop artists who have come out of it, including Aaliyah, Busta Rhymes, Notorious B.I.G., Jay-Z, Big Daddy Kane, Lil' Kim, Mos Def, Talib Kweli, Maino, Fabolous, and Papoose.

up . . . everyone there was poor and trying to get ahead. There was not much hope. You put all those ingredients together, you have people who are willing to do anything at any time. That can't be a safe environment. In each of the buildings there's six floors, four families on each floor, three buildings connected together. Everyone's on top of everybody else. That's a powder keg. Then crack hit around 1985. You had so many people strung out. I mean, everybody. It was an epidemic.

This is not to say that Jay-Z's early life was one of constant sorrow. There were good times, as well. One of his favorite early memories involves himself at the age of four, a bicycle, and an early brush with fame. He told the story in a December 15, 2005, interview with *Rolling Stone*:

I rode this ten-speed. It was really high, but I put my foot through the top bar so I'm ridin' the bike sideways and the whole block is like, oh, God, they couldn't believe this little boy ridin' that bike like that. That was my first feelin' of bein' famous right there. Felt good.

His mother also remembered the incident, and her memory is used in the song "December 4th," on *The Black Album.* "Shawn was a very shy child growing up / He was into sports and a funny story is at 4 he taught his self / How to ride a 2 wheel and isn't that special. . . ."

Being the youngest child, Shawn loved being the center of attention. In fact, even at a young age he was a bit of a show-off, and music was one of the ways he used to get noticed. His parents were both huge music fans and record collectors. Each of them was so proud of their collection that they kept their records labeled separately—some were his mother's, some were his father's, and nobody was allowed to touch any of them without permission.

In this 2005 photograph, Jay-Z poses with some young fans while giving presents to children in his old Bedford-Stuyvesant neighborhood in Brooklyn. Jay-Z grew up in the Marcy Projects section of Bed-Stuy, a poor, crime-ridden neighborhood where drug use was a prominent fixture on the streets.

But Shawn loved Saturdays, when his mother had the day off work and she was home cleaning the house. On those days, she opened the windows and played her favorite soul and funk music over the roar of the vacuum cleaner. Shawn, playing outside, would listen, but in his head, he was already writing different lyrics, making up different rhymes to go with the music. Sometimes, he'd even hear two or three rhymes in his head simultaneously. He'd write them down in his favorite notebook or on whatever scrap of paper was handy.

Jay-Z later remembered the process, quoted in *Jay-Z . . . and the Roc-A-Fella Dynasty*:

> After a while I just started tryin' to write rhymes. I used to be at the table every day for hours. I had this green notebook with no lines in it, and I used to write all crooked. I wrote every . . . day. Then I started running around in the streets, and that's how NOT writing came about. I was comin' up with these ideas, and I'd write 'em on a paper bag, and I had all these paper bags in my pocket, and I hate a lot of things in my pocket, so I started memorizing and holding it.

Shawn's phenomenal memory helped him in school, as well. He was a gifted student and was proud of his intelligence. As he said in *Rolling Stone*, "I just had that feeling of being smart. We did some tests, and I was on a twelfth-grade level. I was crazy happy about that."

Shawn was doing well in school, and he was happy and discovering his love for music. But something was about to happen that would shake his family and him to the core.

LOSS

When Shawn was just eleven years old, his father, Adnis Reeves, left home, never to return. Shawn's mother, an investment company clerk, was now the sole provider for the family of four. Shawn was devastated by his loss and went for years not knowing exactly why his father had abandoned his family. He described his feelings in the *Rolling Stone* interview:

> Kids look up to they pop like Superman. Superman just left the crib? That's traumatic. . . . He was a good guy. It's just that he didn't handle the situation well. He handled it so bad that you forget all the good this guy did. The scorn, the resentment, all the feelings from that, as you can see, I'm a grown-ass man, but it was still there with me.

Being abandoned by his father changed him forever. He discussed this further in the same interview:

> I'd say I changed a little bit. I changed a lot. I became more guarded. I never wanted to be attached to something and get that taken away again. I never wanted to feel that feeling again (of being left). I never wanted to be too happy or gung-ho about something or too mad about something. I just wanted to be cool about it. And it affects my relationships with women. 'Cause even when I was with women I wasn't really with them. In the back of my mind, I'd always feel like "When this breaks up, you know, whatever." So I never really just let myself go.

But despite his loss and grief, he still held on to the few good memories of his father that he had. "He'd take me out and expect me to remember the way we went. When I was five years old, he was teaching me how to navigate through the streets. And then we'd ride in the car and he'd say, 'What size is that woman's dress?' I'd be like, 'Four.' He'd say, 'No, eleven. You gotta pay attention.' And that helps out a lot in raps when I'm talking about the Christian Louboutin and stuff. That's still part of me."

His mother did the best she could to keep the children in school and off the streets. Shawn attended Eli Whitney High School in Brooklyn along with future rapper AZ. After that school closed down, he attended George Washington High School in downtown Brooklyn with two others who would make their own names as rappers—Notorious B.I.G. and Busta Rhymes. Shawn then moved from that school to Trenton Central High School in Trenton, New Jersey, but he did not graduate.

Shawn's mother worried about her son and was anxious to keep him out of trouble. She did everything she could to help him, including encouraging his interest in music. As she says

Two of Jay-Z's classmates at George Washington High School in Brooklyn were future rap artists Notorious B.I.G. *(above)* and Busta Rhymes. Notorious B.I.G. grew up in the Bed-Stuy neighborhood and he too reached great success. Sadly, Notorious B.I.G. died in a 1997 drive-by shooting.

in the song "December 4th," "Shawn used to be in the kitchen beating on the / Table & rapping & um the wee hours of the morning / and then I bought him a boom box & his sisters & brothers / said that he would drive them nuts but that was his way / to keep him close to me & out of trouble."

But despite her best efforts, Shawn began to get into trouble. According to the book *Jay-Z . . . and the Roc-A-Fella Dynasty*, one of the first really serious signs of trouble occurred when Shawn was just twelve. He is quoted as saying, "I uh, shot my brother [Eric] in the shoulder [with] a little gun like a Dillinger. . . . It was a very stupid thing. He was messed up at that time. He'd took a ring of mine. It was very, very foolish you know. . . . I acted outta anger. I was 12. . . . the person who gave me the gun had to be 20 or 21. . . . But I can't blame anybody but myself. . . . [It was] terrible. . . . That's the one thing to this day I regret."

The pressures faced by young African Americans growing up in the projects can be hard to imagine, if you haven't lived through them yourself. And even though Shawn's mother worked full-time to provide for her children, the family was still barely getting by. Surrounded by poverty and hopelessness, anger and violence can seem to be the logical way of dealing with such a life. And when the only people you see with money on a daily basis are those dealing drugs, that way of life can appear more appealing than a life that seems like a trap.

Jay-Z discussed his feelings about this period of his life in the song "December 4th": "But I felt worthless because my shirts didn't match my gear / Now I'm just scratching the surface cause what's buried was a kid torn apart once his pop disappeared / I went to school got good grades could behave when I wanted / But I had demons deep inside that would raise when confronted. . . ."

But, although he was hustling on the streets in his teens, Jay-Z insists that lifestyle only made him stronger. And, he claims that the code of honor among those dealing drugs is stronger than those of high-paid record executives. As he said in an interview quoted in *Jay-Z . . . and the Roc-A-Fella Dynasty*:

> I wouldn't want to grow up no other way. It shaped me, taught me integrity. There's a lot of people in the music business that didn't come from the streets. That's why it's tough for people like us to get along with music executives. We coming from a place where there's integrity, there's honor. There are unwritten rules that people all know. . . . You've got kids that inherited stuff from their parents. They don't appreciate it because it was no work; there's no A to Z, it's just Z. To me, you need somewhere to start, somewhere to be like, "Man, I ain't never going back to not being able to pay my light bill, my stomach growling, eating cereal at night, peanut butter and jelly off the spoon, mayonnaise sandwiches." This is real. I'm talking from a place where if groceries came and we got to put bananas on the cereal, it was a treat.

Shawn's dream was to be a rapper. He met DJ Clark Kent when they were still teenagers. In the *Rolling Stone* interview, Kent recalled his boyhood friend. "When he was fifteen, he wanted to be the best rapper. He was ambitious and he wanted to get better every day. And it's funny how effortlessly it came to him. He's just gifted."

In the same article, Jay's cousin, Be-Hi, who grew up with him in the Marcy Projects, said this about the young Jay-Z: "For years every morning he'd wake up and be in the mirror rhyming to hisself, to hear himself and see how he's pronouncing words and checkin' his flow. Every morning. You know how some people get up and do they calisthenics every morning? That was his thing."

But dreams of becoming a rapper would have to wait. Shawn wanted and needed money *now*, both for himself and for his family, and trying to make it in the music industry was

Photographed above is Jay-Z's childhood friend, DJ Clark Kent. The two met when Jay-Z was a teenager and he was just starting to rap. Clark Kent would later go on to produce tracks for Jay-Z's debut album, *Reasonable Doubt*.

just too big a gamble. Selling drugs, on the other hand, was a sure thing. He felt he had no choice. As he later said, "There was no other way." Much to his mother's sorrow, Shawn left school and started selling drugs and hustling full-time. In *Jay-Z . . . and the Roc-A-Fella Dynasty*, Jay-Z discussed how much he was like every other kid in the neighborhood:

> I'm Shawn Carter, from 5C. I lived in that building right there, the one you live in now. And it can happen for you.

I don't know what it is that you want to do, but something
will happen for you. . . . I could name the ones who did
[have fathers]. There were about three of them in the whole
project. . . . [Growing up without fathers, a boy] learns how
to be a man in the streets. Everyone needs that role model,
that blueprint to guide you through. . . . [For me, that was
hustling] because rap was the real gamble; hustling was the
sure thing. . . .

But although selling drugs was in one sense a "sure thing,"
in other ways, it was a huge gamble. Most who go down that
road end up either dead or in jail. Shawn would need all of his
wits and intelligence to avoid that fate.

Hustling

Although selling drugs seemed like a sure thing compared to trying to make it in the music industry, Shawn was smart enough to know that—at best—it was just a short-term solution to poverty. It's wasn't a long-term career, just a dead-end road. The drug business is far from glamorous, and for most that play the game, the end result is either jail or death. "I've seen this story play out in a million ways," Jay-Z later told *Teen People.*

If Shawn knew that selling drugs wasn't the solution to his problems, why would he do it in the first place? He tried to explain in a later interview, quoted in *Jay-Z . . . and the Roc-A-Fella Records Dynasty*:

> . . . back when I was selling, it was at the height of the crack epidemic, and [a] pretty rough time for everyone, like in—especially—I mean, the neighborhood, it was a—it was a plague in that neighborhood. It was just everywhere, in the hallways. You could smell it in the hallways. . . . Back then it was like—it was—I would say it was like two things. Like, it was either you was doing it or you was moving it. . . .

The one thing Shawn had no intention of doing was using crack. He'd seen what it had done to his brother, Eric. Before crack, Eric had been a popular kid who played basketball. After he discovered crack, he was a whole different person. According to Jay-Z, Eric was trying to steal one of Shawn's rings to support his habit when Shawn shot him. He later said in an interview, "My brother was a really, really, really tough person to get along with. He was messed up on drugs really bad. . . . I didn't know better. [I apologized] right away, and that made it worse [because he forgave me]."

Of course, Shawn did his best not to let his mother know that he was hustling drugs. It's true that, because of the long hours she worked, it was possible not to know exactly what her youngest son was doing, but when the money started coming in and the bills started getting paid, how could she *not* know? Years later, she indicated that she knew the reality of his existence and worried a great deal about him.

As for Shawn, even though he wasn't taking drugs, he was succumbing to another addiction nearly as dangerous—that of fast and easy money, and lots of it. He talked about this deadly addiction in an interview quoted in *Jay-Z and the Roc-A-Fella Dynasty*:

> . . . it starts off as one thing, then it becomes another. In the beginning it's "I gotta take care of my family," but you can't keep saying that, because in your first month, you've changed

their whole situation around. Once you start living "The Life" it's just no stopping. . . . It's completely addictive. . . . I was getting more money than most of the cats—than ALL of that cats I was with.

By his own claims, Shawn was very good at what he was doing. From selling in Brooklyn, his territory rapidly expanded into New Jersey, and even as far away as Virginia. With his growing territory came greater riches, but also a much greater risk of getting arrested, something that constantly weighed on his mind. As a dealer, there was always the chance of getting caught or killed, and with that came the feeling of always looking over one's shoulder. As he said in an interview in *Jay-Z . . . and the Roc-A-Fella Records Dynasty*:

> You never gonna know this feeling, but you could just be driving, absolutely doing nothing, but if you see a cop in the rearview, because you live your life so . . . You do so much dirt every day that you don't even know what's on you. That feeling right there, I hate. I don't ever want to fear another man, ever, ever. But with those cops in the rearview—the lights don't even have to be on.

Years later when he had become a superstar rapper, the situation and the feelings were reversed, as Jay discussed in an interview:

> . . . I was at a restaurant at 145th and Broadway, and the cops came in. . . . This cop was fumbling with his hat because he was so nervous to meet me. . . . Ten years ago he woulda been in my rearview mirror and my heart woulda been beating. But right now he walks in this restaurant. He was a great guy, but the fact that he was so nervous to meet me that he dropped his hat on the floor.

But this was years into Shawn's future. Now, he was making money as a dealer, constantly watching his back and beginning to look for a way out.

LEAVING THE LIFE

Shawn found himself torn between two visions for himself. In one, he would make the risky decision to try to make it as rapper. In the other, he would stay where he was, always fearful but bringing in the big bucks. He would find himself going back and forth between those options for the next several years.

It was in the late 1980s that Shawn, convinced that he was at least as good as—if not better than—any other rapper around, began looking for a way into the music industry. He and rapper Jaz-O, fellow Marcy Project resident, had struck up a friendship. In an interview quoted in *Jay-Z . . . and the Roc-A-Fella Dynasty*, Jay-Z remembered one night when:

> At Gordy Groove's house, Big Daddy Kane, Jaz, and myself were about to put vocals on a tape, a freestyle over a beat Gordy created. Jaz goes first, I go second, Kane goes last. I was inspired and went directly home to write a thousand new and improved rhymes. During the next few months, the tape circulated and the feedback was positive [about] 'the second kid who rapped.' I was taught in my family to believe that anything worth having you had to work extremely hard for. But rap came easy for me. I wouldn't say I took it for granted, but I didn't realize I had a gift until I made that tape.

It was also around this time that Shawn took the name Jay-Z. "I've been more observant than talkative. . . . That's how I got the name 'Jay-Z' from 'Jazzy.' When I was a little kid, I was cool. They used to say back in the day, 'That little kid is jazzy; he's smooth.' That's how I took the 'Jay' and the 'Z.' " (The name 'Jay-Z' is also a reference to the two subway lines, the J and the Z, that rumble through his old neighborhood in Brooklyn.)

When Jay-Z was just starting out as a young rapper, he worked with fellow Bed-Stuy resident and rapper, Big Daddy Kane *(above)*. Jay-Z was featured in Big Daddy Kane's song "Show and Prove."

Jaz-O proved to be a valuable mentor to Jay-Z, teaching him the ins and outs of the recording industry. And when Jaz received a recording contract with EMI, he took Jay-Z along with him to contribute to a song he made called "Hawaiian Sophie," which became a minor hit.

But still, Jay-Z kept hustling, refusing to give it up until he had a record deal of his own. Deep in his heart, he knew that rap offered him the best opportunity to get out of the drug business: "Rap was my way out, the only talent I had, and my shot of making something of myself. And it was legal!"

Even though he went back to selling drugs (after his recording job with Jaz-O), music was becoming his main focus. He described this in an interview cited in *Jay-Z . . . and the Roc-A-Fella Dynasty*:

> Even though I was back on the street, my heart was still in music. I was preoccupied with numbers, weight, and my business, but my mind was flooded with ideas about songs, hooks, and verses. When my thoughts began to crowd each other, I would go to the corner store, get a pen, and empty my head, pouring rhymes onto pieces of paper bags. But how many scraps can you fit in your pocket? I had to start memorizing my ideas until I got home, which was usually in the wee hours of the morning.
>
> Ironically, using memorization to hold on to my lines is the way I developed the writing style I use today. No pen, paper, or paper bags needed. Just point out the track and I'm all over it. . . . And yet . . . I also became fully committed to putting my hustle down. I kept moving further south—from Trenton, NJ, to Maryland, and finally to Virginia. I spent less and less time in New York, but when I did come home, I would go to parties and jump on the mike, freestyling here and there.

Knowing that selling drugs would never be enough to get him and his family out of the projects, Jay-Z constantly worked on honing his craft—his rhymes, his flow, everything that went into the technique of rapping. He also knew from the beginning that the subject of his raps would be his life and the lives of others like him living in poverty in the projects. According to *Jay-Z . . . and the Roc-A-Fella Records Dynasty*, he knew that his goal as a rapper would be "to have a conversation with the

BIG DADDY KANE

While to some he's best known as the man who gave Jay-Z his start, Big Daddy Kane (born Antonio Hardy) is considered by many to be one of the best rappers in the history of hip-hop.

Through such albums as *Long Live the Kane, It's a Big Daddy Thing*, and *Looks Like a Job For . . .* , he became renowned for his ability to syncopate over faster hip-hop beats. Indeed, despite suffering from asthma, he is acknowledged as one of the pioneering masters of fast-rap. He is equally known for his sense of style, setting a number of fashion trends in the late 1980s and early 1990s, including high-top fades, velour suits, and four-finger rings.

He is still a prominent force in music, collaborating with groups such as Jurassic 5, releasing new songs, and receiving recognition at the VH1 Hip-Hop Honors. Known for having one of the sharpest flows and deliveries of any MC, he, alongside Kool G Rap and Rakim, is considered by many to be one of the greatest influences in all of hip-hop history. When MTV ranked Big Daddy Kane the seventh greatest MC of all time, Ice-T wrote, "To me, Big Daddy Kane is still today one of the best rappers. I would put Big Daddy Kane against any rapper in a battle. Jay-Z, Nas, Eminem, any of them. . . . I may out-dress him, but I'm not going to try to out-rap him. Big Daddy Kane can rap circles around cats."

world . . . I'm telling the world my plight. I was speaking about the people and neighborhoods and mentality of someone who comes from nothing. . . . I didn't want to sell drugs. I wanted a better life."

Searching for that better life, he appeared on a few records, including "Can I Get Open" with members from Original Flavor, a now forgotten trio of rappers from New York. He began to attract a small following with the release of the song "Show and Prove," which featured Big Daddy Kane and several other rappers. Although none of these releases exactly hit it big, the work enabled him to meet and make contacts with other people in the recording industry. But until he was able to get the recording deal *he* wanted, he wasn't about to give up the money that dealing drugs provided. He would soon meet the man who would help to make a record deal possible.

DAMON DASH

Damon Dash was born wanting to be an entrepreneur. He grew up in Manhattan, in a middle-class section of Harlem. Compared to Shawn, he had a relatively privileged childhood and was able to attend prep schools in Manhattan and Connecticut with the assistance of need-based and academic scholarships. He lived in two worlds, moving from the streets of Harlem to the privileged private schools of the white upper class. As he once said in an interview quoted in *Jay-Z . . . and the Roc-A-Fella Dynasty,* "Do you know how hard it was to come back to my neighborhood in penny loafers with khaki pants and a blazer? I had two lives. My uptown life was in Harlem. My downtown was P.S. 6 on 81st and Park Avenue. Then I went to [the Dwight School]. So I got to see both sides. Taught me a lot."

One of the things he quickly absorbed was the interest that whites living in the suburbs had in the black culture of the streets and projects. "I was amused to see how rich folks were intrigued by what was going on in the streets . . . [and decided, in the future, I would do something business-wise] to market

Pictured above is Jay-Z's onetime friend and business associate, Damon Dash. Jay-Z, Damon Dash, and Kareem "Biggs" Burke co-founded Roc-A-Fella Records in 1996. After Jay-Z and Dash had a falling out, Dash sold his share of Roc-A-Fella Records in 2004 and founded The Damon Dash Music Group.

the streets [to both]. . . . I needed a business where I could have fun and make money."

So when Dash received his GED in 1988, he became "an entrepreneur, hustling to get money in any way. I went to some parties and noticed the easy lifestyle of the MCs, with no repercussions, so I wanted to have money and enjoy life."

Early in his career, Dash had ambitions of using hip-hop culture to set up businesses in music, fashion, and marketing. By utilizing what is known as cross-marketing, he could use the hip-hop artists he signed to sell clothes, cars, and any other product available. In other words, this would allow him to use hip-hop culture to make money off every aspect of the culture. As Dash explained in a 2004 interview with *Fortune Small Business*, "We (the hip-hop community) shouldn't let other people make money off of us, and we shouldn't give free advertising with our lifestyle." For example, when the legendary rap group Run-DMC became known for wearing Adidas sneakers, sales of those sneakers skyrocketed, making money only for Adidas. But if a rap artist were to wear sneakers of his own clothing line, he (and the company) would make the profits.

Dash began moving into the world of artist management, hoping to find the artist that would allow him to achieve his dreams. It was at this time that he met Jay-Z through their mutual friend DJ Clark Kent. It was a perfect match: two ambitious men, both wanting to achieve the same goals.

There was some initial trepidation before their first meeting; guys from Harlem like Dash didn't hang with guys like Jay-Z from Brooklyn, but the two hit it off immediately. As Dash remembered it in *Jay-Z . . . and the Roc-A-Fella Records Dynasty*, " . . . I went to Brooklyn to meet Jay at French Gordon's studio, and that was big, because back then cats from Harlem didn't go to Brooklyn. When I met the dude the first thing that I noticed was that he was wearing a pair of Nike Airs and that was something that only cats from Harlem were into, and he was wearing them right—he had them laced right and everything. That's when I knew he was a cool dude. We became friends from there. . . . people from Harlem and Brooklyn seem to have crazy stereotypes about one another. But we became good friends. . . ."

They became not only good friends, but business associates. Dash signed Jay to a management deal in 1995. Later, another friend, Kareem "Biggs" Burke joined them as a partner. But a management deal wasn't the same as having a record contract. And until Jay got that, he was reluctant to give up the lifestyle that drug money provided him. He knew, though, that it was time to leave the streets. As he remembered, quoted in *Jay-Z* by Geoff Barnes, "By the age of 22 I knew I had to get out [of the drug business] because the only future is jail or die." Now all he needed was a record contract to make that possible. But getting a contract would prove more difficult than he hoped.

On His Own Terms

You've got to have confidence to believe that you can do it. I mean, because when those doors were shut for me as far as, you know, someone signing me to a record label and putting out my material, I could have easily said, that's it, you know. I'm not good enough, this is not for me, you know, but I didn't do that.

—*Jay-Z . . . and the Roc-A-Fella Dynasty*

Throughout 1995, Jay-Z, along with Dash and the rest of the team, began recording tracks for what would eventually become his debut album, *Reasonable Doubt*. Wanting his debut album to be special, he enlisted (as he would do with future albums) other talented performers to help. His old friend DJ Clark Kent provided beats and also produced several songs. And, a soon-to-be-legendary rapper from Brooklyn, Christopher George Latore Wallace, also known as Biggie Smalls or Notorious B.I.G., joined Jay-Z on the track "Brooklyn's Finest."

Jay-Z had known Biggie since high school, but working together allowed them to cement their friendship. Biggie's influence as a rapper was enormous, and even today, he is considered by many to be among the best MCs ever.

Once the album was completed, Dash worked to find a record company to distribute it to stores. Jay-Z's and his team's first move was to record and press copies of the single "In My Lifetime." They sold records out of the trunk of a car, but were still unable to get radio play. Based on the stir that the single caused, however, local New York independent label Payday Records picked up the single for distribution.

Jay-Z signed a deal with Payday, but when the company failed to live up to its promises, he walked out. Taking the payout money that the company owed him, he, Dash, and Kareem Burke started their own record company—Roc-A-Fella Records—to distribute his debut album themselves.

ROC-A-FELLA RECORDS

The newly formed company came to an arrangement with Priority Records to distribute the album to stores. The album eventually went gold, but this success led the group to regret giving the rights of their album away to a major record company. Instead, they began looking for a way to use Jay-Z in order to become a major record company themselves.

Finally, they found what they were looking for, and signed a deal with Def Jam Records. Def Jam was famous throughout the hip-hop world for promoting some of the most famous rap artists in the world, including Run-DMC, LL Cool Jay, and Public Enemy. Based solely on the critical acclaim of Jay-Z's

Confidence and tenacity helped Jay-Z break out of the pack of aspiring rappers. Although he is one of the most talented artists in the industry, it is his belief in himself and his willingness to persevere that have made him a success.

debut album, Def Jam entered into a joint venture with Roc-A-Fella. Under the agreement, everything, including ownership of the masters (the original audio recordings) would be split 50/50 between the two companies. With this deal, Jay-Z would be able to become a professional rapper with all the control over his career that he wanted, and he would finally be able to give up drug dealing forever.

In an interview quoted in *Jay-Z . . . and the Roc-A-Fella Dynasty*, Jay-Z explained exactly how the deal with Def Jam came about:

> My dream when I did *Reasonable Doubt* was to do one album. I thought I was being artistic, making a statement. But when we sat down with Russell Simmons and Lyor Cohen to negotiate with Def Jam, I was the only artist on Roc-A-Fella that could close the deal. They were only interested in us because of the heat from *Reasonable*. So once that contract was signed, I knew I would be in the vocal booth for another five to seven albums. . . . I never waited for anybody to give me anything. If I wanted something I knew that I was going to have to be the one to go out and get it. . . . Opportunities didn't come my way. I had to chase them. I finally caught one. . . . In my heart, I always wanted someone else to do it. I wanted to be the businessman.

He may have wanted to be the businessman, but *Reasonable Doubt* proved him to be a true hip-hop artist with unlimited potential. *Vibe* magazine said of the album, "*Reasonable Doubt* may arguably be one of the most misunderstood albums in hip-hop, [but] its critics cannot deny its classic presence." And AllMusic.com gave the album five stars, saying:

> . . . he was a street hustler from the projects who rapped about what he knew . . . and was very, very good at it . . . an instant classic of a debut, detailing his experiences on the

streets with disarming honesty, and writing some of the most acrobatic rhymes heard in quite some time. Parts of the persona that Jay-Z would ride to superstardom are already in place: He's cocky bordering on arrogant, but playful and witty, and exudes an effortless, unaffected cool

NOTORIOUS B.I.G.

He was born Christopher George Latore Wallace on May 21, 1972. He was dead before he was 24, murdered by an unknown killer in Los Angeles on March 9, 1997. But in his brief life, he established himself as one of hip-hop's greatest rappers.

Wallace was popularly known as Biggie Smalls (after a gangster in the 1975 film *Let's Do It Again*), Big Poppa, Frank White (from the film *King of New York*), and by his primary stage name, Notorious B.I.G. (Business Instead of Game). He recorded just two albums during his lifetime (*Ready to Die* in 1994 and *Life After Death*, released just fifteen days after his death) and was known for his "loose easy flow," dark semi-autobiographical lyrics, and mesmerizing storytelling abilities.

Despite his brief career, his influence and popularity remain undiminished. In 2003, when *XXL* magazine asked many hip-hop artists to list their five favorite MCs, Biggie's name appeared more than anyone else's. In 2006, he was ranked at number three on MTV's list of the Greatest MCs of All Time.

Since his death, his lyrics have been sampled and quoted by a vast array of hip-hop, R & B, and pop artists, including Jay-Z, 50 Cent, Nas, Fat Joe, Nelly, Pharrell Williams, Lil' Wayne, Ludacris, Big Pun, Beanie Sigel, Usher, Ashanti, Alicia Keys, and Nelly Furtado. Through them and through his records, Biggie's legacy lives on.

throughout . . . the brief "22 Two's" . . . demonstrates Jay-Z's extraordinary talent as a pure free-style rapper . . . songs like "D'Evils" and "Regrets" are some of the most personal and philosophical he's ever recorded. It's that depth that helps *Reasonable Doubt* rank as one of the finest albums of New York's hip-hop renaissance of the '90s.

Lyrically, the songs fit into the genre, or style, of rap known as gangsta rap or Mafioso rap. These songs examine life on the streets for a dealer, kingpin, or street hustler. By rapping about what he knew, about his own life, Jay-Z was able to turn his personal experiences into art. As he reflected in an interview quoted in *Jay-Z . . . and the Roc-A-Fella Dynasty*:

> My first album, *Reasonable Doubt*, was about what I knew best: hustling. I felt like other rappers had touched on the subject, but I wanted every hustler that I ever knew to feel like I had been reading his diary. I wanted to write an album that was honest about the glamour and materialism, because living large was real for us. But I also wanted to talk about the depression, the drama, the sacrifices, and the pain that come with the street life. I made that album like it was my first and last.

EAST VERSUS WEST

Even though Jay-Z had left the life of the street behind, that didn't guarantee that he'd left the threat of violence behind with it. For years, rappers in different parts of the country had developed their own unique styles of rap, with bragging rights over who was the best up for grabs. But during the mid-1990s, the rivalry between two record labels on opposite coasts of the country raised the competition to new heights. The tension and competition between West Coast rappers and East Coast rappers reached a new high in 1996.

On September 7, 1996, Tupac Shakur *(above)* was shot four times in a drive-by shooting, and six days later on September 13, he passed away. His murder and the murder of his rival, Notorious B.I.G., remain unsolved.

The rivalry centered on two of the hip-hop world's biggest stars: Tupac Shakur, who signed with Los Angeles-based Death Row Records, was one half of the feud; Notorious B.I.G., Bad Boy Records' star and Jay-Z's friend, represented the East Coast.

At first, the battle was fought through their music, as the two traded insults via their songs. But things took an ugly turn on November 30, 1994, when Tupac was shot five times while leaving a recording studio in New York. He believed that Bad Boy Records, run by Sean "Puffy" Combs, and Biggie were

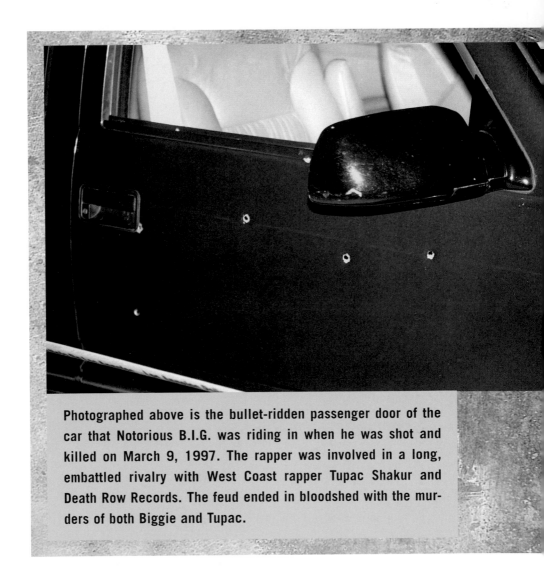

Photographed above is the bullet-ridden passenger door of the car that Notorious B.I.G. was riding in when he was shot and killed on March 9, 1997. The rapper was involved in a long, embattled rivalry with West Coast rapper Tupac Shakur and Death Row Records. The feud ended in bloodshed with the murders of both Biggie and Tupac.

responsible. And although they denied any involvement, Biggie's song "Who Shot Ya?" did little to settle the mounting feud.

In 1995, Tupac released his song, "Hit 'Em Up," which insulted not only Notorious B.I.G. and Bad Boy Records, but almost every other New York rapper he felt had aligned himself with Biggie, including Jay-Z. Ironically, by bringing Jay-Z into the feud and rapping lyrics like "I'm a Bad Boy killa, Jay-Z die too!" Tupac inadvertently helped to raise Jay-Z's status within the rap community.

The war of words continued until, perhaps inevitably, it erupted into deadly violence. On September 7, 1996, Tupac Shakur was shot and killed. On March 8, 1997, Notorious B.I.G. met the same fate. To this date, both crimes remain unsolved. With these two deaths, the violence sometimes glamorized in gangsta rap suddenly became a little too real, and many artists retreated from it.

Jay-Z was devastated by the death of Biggie, his friend and fellow rapper. As he recalled in *Jay-Z . . . and the Roc-A-Fella Dynasty*:

> . . . going to Big's funeral was a big deal to me. I don't go to funerals period. I don't want that to be my last memory of them. . . . We knew each other at Westinghouse High School. We'd see each other, and we'd nod. Then we both was in the music business, and we always said, "We gotta hook up and do something together." Finally we did "Brooklyn's Finest." That's when we clicked. I sat there, he sat there. I was like "Yo, you need a pen?" No pen. That's how I make my music, too. It was crazy, it was ill for me. . . . I can't even describe what that loss was like for me. It was worse than someone losing someone in a drug game, because you know that's the risk you take when you get into the streets—death or jail. This was supposed to be music.

With the deaths of Tupac Shakur and Notorious B.I.G., the rap throne was unoccupied. One album, no matter how strong, was not enough to raise Jay-Z to the top of the hip-hop heap. He returned to the recording studio and continued to build on his initial success.

In My Lifetime

Entering the recording studio to record his second album, *In My Lifetime, Vol. 1,* Jay-Z was still reeling from the death of his friend Biggie. In some ways, that tragedy inspired him to go on, as he said in an interview quoted in *Jay-Z . . . and the Roc-A-Fella Dynasty*:

> I recorded my second album after Big was murdered. . . . I felt Big had elevated rhyming to heights not seen in hip-hop, and that it would be selfish for me to retire. My staying in the game is like a promise I made to Big. He had done so much to represent New York that I didn't want us to return to that time. . . . when it seemed like New York hip-hop didn't even matter anymore.

The album was produced by Sean Combs, and upon its release in September 1997, it sold even better than *Reasonable Doubt*. While the first album was a gritty, hard-core look at street life, the new album was criticized by many fans of the first album for being too smooth and "pop." One executive acknowledged the album's change of focus, telling *Billboard* magazine that "The overall strategy is to increase [Jay-Z's] visibility and make him that crossover artist without sacrificing his full street credibility." But in the eyes of many hard-core rap fans, it was a sellout, giving up authenticity in the hope of greater sales.

Despite the album's heavier pop overtones, critics still praised both the record and Jay-Z's rapidly improving skills as a rapper, with AllMusic.com saying:

> After the death of friend and compatriot the Notorious B.I.G. in early 1997, Jay-Z made his claim for the title of best rapper on the East Coast (or anywhere) with his sophomore shot, *In My Lifetime, Vol. 1*. Though the productions are just a bit flashier and more commercial than on his debut, Jay-Z remained the tough street rapper, and even improved a bit on his flow, already one of the best in hip-hop. Still showing his roots in the Marcy projects . . . Jay-Z struts the line between project poet and up-and-coming player, and manages to have it both ways. He slings some of the most cutting rhymes in hip-hop . . . ("If I shoot you, I'm brainless / but if you shoot me, then you're famous"). . . . Having one of the toughest producers around (Premier) as well as one of the slickest (Puff Daddy/P. Diddy) sometimes creates a disconnect between who Jay-Z is and who he wants to become, but he balances both personas with the best rapping heard in the rap game since the deaths of 2Pac and Notorious B.I.G.

On *In My Lifetime, Vol. 1*, Jay-Z, for the first time, addresses a problem faced by many successful rappers. Once they

On November 4, 1997, Jay-Z released his sophomore album, *In My Lifetime, Vol. 1*, which was produced by Sean Combs *(above)*. *In My Lifetime* was criticized for not having the same edge as his first release, *Reasonable Doubt*. Many critics complained that *In My Lifetime, Vol. 1* had a glossier, pop sound.

leave life on the streets and poverty for the life of celebrity and success, how can they keep their problems and lives relevant to their audiences? In other words, these fans were first attracted to Jay-Z because of the stories of his life and problems as a hustler. Could they still care about the problems of a multimillionaire?

He deals with this in the song "Lucky Me," saying "Every day I'm dealing with stress / Got up out the streets, you'd think a [person] could rest / Can't even enjoy myself at party unless I'm out on the dance floor / [wearing a bulletproof] vest."

Jay-Z also did his part to help end the feud between East and West Coast rappers by collaborating with West Coast rapper Too $hort. By reaching out to his West Coast rival, he hoped to at least lower the level of tension between the two coasts. And by saying in the song "I want Biggie to rest in peace, as well as Pac," he acknowledged that both men were equally worthy of respect.

But while trying to bank the fires of the ongoing East Coast/West Coast feud, Jay makes his initial claim to the East Coast throne in the song "The City Is Mine," saying, "Jay-Z, Roc-A-Fella, yo, know the name / I ain't a player get it right, I'm controlling the game / From now until they blow holes in my frame / I'ma stand firm, holdin my aim, feel me? / I'm the focal point like Biggie in his prime/on the low though—shhhhh, the city is mine!"

Although he was staking his claim to the throne, Jay-Z still felt pressure to defend the album against critics, saying that it simply revealed other sides to his personality. In later years, he acknowledged that the album was too pop-oriented. In an interview on YES Network's "CenterStage with Michael Kay" show, he said that if he could do just one thing over in his career, it would be *Vol. 1*, claiming that "it [the CD] was *this* close to being a classic, but I put like, a few songs on there that ruined it." It has been widely speculated that the songs he was referring to were "I Know What Girls Like" and "(Always Be My) Sunshine."

In the winter of 1997 and early spring of 1998, Jay-Z set out on his first major tour, becoming the opening act of Puff Daddy's No Way Out arena tour. His stay was short-lived, though, as he soon left the tour. He says in *Jay-Z . . . and the Roc-A-Fella Records Dynasty*, "to support *Vol. 1*, I went on tour with Puff and Bad Boy. I swallowed my pride and opened for him, but by the middle of the tour I felt like I was taking too much of a loss. I went to Puff and told him I respected what he was doing, but I had to leave."

Returning to New York, Jay helped finish shooting Roc-A-Fella Films' first release, *Streets Is Watching*, named after the

SEAN COMBS

He is one of the most recognized brand names in the entertainment industry. He's a business man, record producer, actor, and rapper. Previously known as Puff Daddy and later as P. Diddy, today he is known to the world simply as Diddy.

He rules over a media empire that includes the record label Bad Boy Records, the clothing lines Sean John and Sean by Sean Combs, a movie production company, and two restaurants. He has taken on the roles of recording executive, performer, producer of the MTV series *Making the Band*, writer, arranger, clothing designer, film actor (*Monster's Ball* and *Made)* and Broadway actor (*A Raisin in the Sun)*. As of 2007, Diddy is thought to be the richest hip-hop entertainer, with a net worth of more than $346 million.

While criticized by some as trying to be too many things to too many people and for watering down and overly commercializing hip-hop for a mainstream market, Diddy remains fearless; he is always ready to take a chance and try something new.

single from Jay's second album. The movie, which was released straight to video, was shot entirely at Marcy Projects and starred many of the members of the Team-ROC artistic roster, including DJ Clue, the R & B group Christion, and Memphis Bleek. The film received strong reviews, with VH1.com saying, "realism pervades within the framework of this music video, or 'videomentary,' about street life . . . (offering) a realistic view of his neighborhood without the commercial flash of over-the-top rap displays." The film helped to solidify the reputation of both Jay-Z and Roc-A-Fella as being "the real thing," and the true representatives of life in the 'hood.

With the success of both *In My Lifetime, Vol. 1.*, and *Streets Is Watching*, Jay's career was obviously on the rise. His next album would take him straight to the top.

IT'S A HARD KNOCK LIFE

On September 29, 1998, Jay-Z released his third solo album, *Vol. 2 . . . Hard Knock Life*. Propelled by the crossover smash single, "Hard Knock Life (Ghetto Anthem)," it became his biggest selling album, selling more than 5 million copies to date and debuting at number one on *Billboard* magazine's pop chart.

The single "Hard Knock Life (Ghetto Anthem)" was heard on radio stations coast-to-coast, by audiences both black and white. The blueprint of the song was simple yet ingenious. It used the chorus from the song "It's a Hard Knock Life" from the Broadway smash-hit musical *Annie*. The lyrics from the song, sung in the original musical by young girls in an orphanage ("It's the Hard Knock Life for us / It's the Hard Knock life for us / Stead of treated, we get tricked / Stead of kisses, we get kicked / It's the Hard Knock Life"), take on a whole new meaning in the Jay-Z version.

As www.music.com put it, "At his best, he shows no fear—witness how the title track shamelessly works a Broadway showstopper from *Annie* into a raging ghetto cry, yet keeps it smooth enough for radio. . . . it's a stunning single." With lyrics like "I flow for chicks wishin' they ain't have to strip to pay tuition," and "I don't know how to sleep, I gotta eat / stay on my toes / Got a lot of beef so logically I prey on my foes / Hustlin' still inside of me and as far as progress / You'd be hard-pressed to find another rapper hot as me. . . ." Jay-Z brilliantly takes the tale of Depression-era orphans and transforms it into a rapper's rags-to-riches saga.

Other singles released from the album were also successful. Produced by such hip-hop luminaries as Timbaland, Kid Capri, and Just Blaze, "Jigga What," "Money Ain't a Thing," and "Can I Get a . . ." ruled the charts both in the United States and abroad, and firmly established Jay-Z as one of hip-hop's preeminent rappers. Jay-Z himself was proud of the album saying in *Jay-Z and the Roc-A-Fella Records Dynasty* that "I was in a zone when I did that album, completely focused, completely creative."

But despite the album's overwhelming popular success, many critics gave it lukewarm reviews, complaining that by striving for greater commercial acceptance, Jay-Z had compromised both the quality and complexity of his music. Another criticism that many had of the album was the number of guest stars that Jay-Z used. With help from Memphis Bleek, Amil & Big Jaz, DMX, Ja Rule, Too $hort, and Jermaine Dupri, Jay rapped solo on only two of the album's fourteen tracks.

Nonetheless, the album went on to win numerous awards, including the Grammy Award for best rap album. Jay-Z boycotted the awards. In an interview quoted in *Jay-Z . . . and the Roc-A-Fella Dynasty*, he said, "I am boycotting the Grammy Awards because too many major rap artists continue to be overlooked. . . . Rappers deserve more attention from the Grammy committee and from the whole world."

Winning an award and refusing to attend the ceremony only served to enhance his reputation with both the artistic establishment and the hard-core hip-hop community. His next major achievement, the Hard Knock Life Tour, would prove his preeminence as a hip-hop artist.

Put together to help promote the album *Hard Knock Life*, the tour hit 52 cities in the United States and sold out in each one. As Jay-Z described it in an interview, "When we put together the Hard Knock Life Tour . . . I wanted to make history. First of all, we brought together artists like X, Red, Ja, Eve, Beans, Bleek and the whole family. And then, after selling out 52 stadiums across America without one incident of violence, we knew we had reopened the possibility of stadium-sized, hardcore hip-hop tours."

To the outside world, the life of a musician on tour seems like a life of nothing but fun. But Jay pointed out just how exhausting that kind of tour can be, "(On that tour), every day was tiring. Every day was like [the movie] 'Groundhog Day' . . . you know, every day the same thing over and over again. But once I touched the stage, it was like I was doing it the first night, because the energy was just incredible, and then for it to be sold out all over the place . . . it was a magical ride."

ROCAWEAR

Indeed, Jay-Z was on a magical ride. He had a smash-hit album and singles, a sold-out tour, and a Grammy Award. But not content with simply being a music icon, he and Roc-A-Fella Records began to expand their business empire.

The company established its Rocawear clothing line, going back to the original idea of cross-marketing. As Damon Dash explained in an interview quoted in *Jay-Z . . . and the Roc-A-Fella Dynasty*, "I came in with the same concept. . . . I'm not licensing to you. I want to half own the company. . . . I may not know how to manufacture and design clothing, but I have a brand that I can bring to it." Going into partnership with New York-based clothing manufacturer Comet, Rocawear received a 50/50 split on all profits earned by the clothing.

Vol 2 . . . Hard Knock Life was Jay-Z's highest selling album to date, with approximately 5 million records sold in the United States and 8 million records sold worldwide. The success of the album confirmed Jay-Z's role as a prominent rap star. In the photograph above, Jay-Z *(far right)* poses with fellow rappers at the announcement of the Hard Knock Life Tour in 1999.

And, of course, Jay-Z would be the company's preeminent model. As he explained, "When you're a kid, you want to wear the clothes all the other kids are wearing. Then you get a little money, you want to show off. So you buy a nice piece of jewelry. I guess needing to show off never fades. . . . I guess the style I have now has a lot to do with what's going on out there in the streets. . . . I'll always be in style. . . ."

Also contributing to the company's profits was a whole new generation of rappers added to the recording label. These artists, including new stars such as Beanie Sigel and Freeway, appeared with Jay-Z in videos and on tour, always wearing Rocawear clothing. The success of the artists helped to sell the clothes, and the success of the clothes helped to sell the artists. All of which combined to make Jay-Z and his partners very rich men. Everything was going according to plan. But, sometimes plans have a way of going horribly awry.

AN ERUPTION OF VIOLENCE

On December 2, 1999, Jay-Z performed at New York club Irving Plaza to promote his forthcoming album, *Vol. 3: Life and Times of S. Carter.* After the event, he and some friends went to the Kit Kat Klub in Times Square for an industry party celebrating the new album, *Amplified,* by rapper Q-Tip of the group A Tribe Called Quest. Upon entering the club, Jay-Z was informed that also attending the party was his rival, Lance "Un" Rivera, the CEO of Undeas Entertainment. It was widely rumored that Rivera was the man behind a large bootlegging operation that sold illegal copies of Jay-Z's recordings. (To date, Rivera has vehemently denied this charge.)

Reports of what actually happened that night are conflicted and confused. What is known for certain is that a fight broke out in the VIP section of the club. When it was over, Un had been stabbed in the stomach and shoulder. According to some reports, Jay-Z had approached Un, but instead of saying "hello," plunged a knife into his stomach, and whispered into his ear, "You broke my heart."

Un recovered from his wounds and filed a civil suit, claiming that Jay-Z had been his attacker. In addition to the civil

Jay-Z is taken to the police precinct after being handcuffed and arrested for the stabbing of record executive Lance "Un" Rivera at a New York City club. Jay-Z initially denied the incident and claimed he was nowhere near Rivera when he was stabbed. But, Jay-Z later pleaded guilty to a misdemeanor assault charge and received three years probation.

lawsuit, which would force Jay-Z to pay monetary damages if he were convicted, New York prosecutors made the decision to file criminal charges against him for assault. If convicted, he faced up to fifteen years in prison. His career was in danger of ending as quickly as it had begun.

Violence and Art

The prosecutors in the criminal charges against Jay-Z subpoenaed witnesses from the Kit Kat Klub to try and back up their charges. Jay maintained his innocence, claiming that a video that had been taken at the club would prove that he had been nowhere near Un at the time of the stabbing.

But as the civil suit commenced in 2000, Un's story began to change. He stated that he was really no longer certain that it was Jay-Z who had stabbed him. Because of this, the prosecutors in the case began to be more and more uncertain about how strong their charges against Jay-Z were.

It took two years to resolve the issue. Un eventually withdrew his civil complaint, which, according to the Associated Press, was settled out of court for between $500,000 and

Pictured above is record producer, Lance "Un" Rivera. On December 2, 1999, Rivera was was involved in a fight at a club in New York City and was stabbed. Jay-Z was arrested for the assault and pleaded guilty to a misdemeanor assault charge.

$1,000,000. But Jay-Z was still facing a criminal trial and the prospect of jail. The prosecutors offered Jay-Z a plea agreement. They told Jay-Z that if he would plead guilty to a lesser misdemeanor charge, he would receive no jail time, but three years of probation. Jay-Z accepted the offer, stating that he just did not feel comfortable taking the risk of going to prison, simply to prove his innocence.

He was aware that it is sometimes difficult for African-American men to receive equal justice in the United States. Growing up in the projects, he'd seen this too much. As he said in a interview in *People* magazine, "Where I grew up, I saw a lot of people get wronged. No matter how much you believe in the truth, that's always in the back of your mind."

It is ironic that having avoided prison while a drug dealer, he came close to doing jail time as one of America's most successful hip-hop artists. The experience changed his way of thinking, as he explained in an interview quoted in *Jay-Z . . . and the Roc-A-Fella Dynasty*:

> That was the turning point for me. . . . It was like, O.K., this can all go away fast. You work hard for years, and it can all go away in a night. Slow down, big boy. Think . . . I think that was a wake-up call and a calling card for me that that—to let me know, like, it could just all go down the drain. Like it can all be taken away from you . . . I felt like I was untouchable, but that let me see that it could all go away in an instant, it made me more careful.

Despite the pressure of civil and criminal charges against him, Jay-Z continued to release and record new albums. Just three weeks after the incident at the Kit Kat Klub, his fourth album, *Vol. III: Life and Times of S. Carter*, debuted at number one on the *Billboard* charts. The first single, "Big Pimpin'" combined a commercial, pop-sounding production with lyrics glorifying a life of disrespecting women. It was a huge success.

Critics and fans loved the album, noticing the careful balance that Jay struck between satisfying both his hard-core and his more "pop" fans. *Daily* said that "few hip-hop artists can balance staying true to the streets and go platinum at the same time; Jay-Z happens to be one of them. Jay-Z sells records, not his soul." And *Rolling Stone* said:

> . . . on his fourth album . . . he's a sweet contradiction. Lyrically . . . he's more misogynous [showing a hatred or fear of women] than ever. But he . . . has become a better architect of songs. This is his strongest album to date, with music that's filled with catchy hooks, rump-shaking beats and lyrics fueled by Jay's hustler's vigilance. On the Timbaland-produced "Come and Get Me"—an exhilarating piece of craftsmanship where two separate . . . licks are joined by a valley of babbling brooks, tropical birds and church bells—Jay describes fear and loathing at the top of the hip-hop heap, with phenomenal results: "Went on MTV with do-rags / I made them love you . . . I expect to hear, 'Jay, if it wasn't for you' / But instead all I hear is fussin' in your crew / How y'all schemin', tryin' to get accustomed to my moves. . . ."

Jay-Z stayed busy throughout the summer of 2000, contributing to the soundtrack of *The Nutty Professor II: The Klumps,* and appearing on Busta Rhymes's *Anarchy* album, on the song "Why We Die." Later that summer, Roc-A-Fella Films released its second film, *Backstage,* documenting the 1999 Hard Knock Life Tour.

The film performed respectably at the box office, but that same summer, the company's clothing line, Rocawear, really took off, growing from sales of $8,000,000 in 1999 to $150,000,000 in the year 2000.

Nobody would have been surprised if Jay-Z took the time to settle back and enjoy his good fortune, but he still had too much to say. He said in an interview quoted in *Jay-Z . . . and the Roc-A-Fella Dynasty* that he kept recording because he had,

> . . . something to talk about. People want to hear the struggle, the story. They want to hear something they can relate to. . . . You know, I have a struggle right now: my struggle to maintain my own identity in the midst of all this. . . . Somebody told me the other day that no matter where you are, there you are. You put me in a big car, you put a couple of chains on me, and you put me in a room with Mariah (Carey), I'm still the same person. . . . So even above and beyond it being good music, there's something else there, some substance. . . . I'm an artist. I like to be creative. I like to make music and I like to get the reaction from people after they have heard the music. . . . I want to make music. I want people to relate to my story. . . .

Jay-Z continued to tell his story on his next album, *The Dynasty: Roc La Familia*, released on October 25, 2000. The album, which reached number one on the charts by year's end, marked the first time in 25 years that one artist had had two number-one albums in the same year.

Although marketed as a "Jay-Z" record, the album served mainly to promote other talent on the Roc-A-Fella label. Critical response was mixed, and many fans were disappointed that Jay-Z's labelmates were more evident on the album than Jay-Z himself.

Even though on many songs Jay-Z only spat out a lyric or two before turning the mic over to other talents, critics did mention that several of the songs, including "This Can't Be Life," and "Where Have You Been," were among his finest accomplishments as a songwriter. In addition, *Rolling Stone* noted the dual roles that Jay assumed, "half floss-king still thugging it, half street teacher offering warnings and experience to those who have ears to hear."

It is on the song "Where Have You Been," performed by Jay-Z and Beanie Sigel, that Jay-Z makes his first recorded reference to his father leaving his life, saying, "But I ain't mad at you, Dad / Holla at your lad."

To many fans and critics, though, *The Dynasty: Roc La Familia* was just Jay-Z marking time until his next "real" album. Little did they know that his next album would be considered by many as his best album to date.

THE BLUEPRINT

Before he could get to work, other legal issues arose. Throughout the spring of 2001, the New York Police Department, attempting to crack down on violence within the hip-hop community, began close surveillance of nightclubs frequented by celebrity musicians, among other tactics.

One night in April, police claimed that they saw Jay-Z's bodyguard retrieve a gun from the front passenger seat of a car parked in front of the Manhattan club Club Exit. Moments after the car drove off with Jay-Z and two other men inside, the police pulled the car over and found a loaded gun in the bodyguard's waistband. Under New York law, if police find a gun inside a car, everyone in the car can be charged with possessing that gun, although in practice that kind of prosecution rarely occurs.

Not this time though. Jay-Z was charged with criminal possession of a gun in the third degree. Although the charges were eventually dropped, it was just one more legal hassle—and one more issue that Jay-Z was able to utilize in recording his next album.

When it was time for him to enter the studio, he was on a roll. All the problems and stresses, as well as the triumphs, of the past year came out; nine tracks were recorded in just two days—a remarkable achievement.

The album would be entitled *The Blueprint*. It was released on September 11, 2001, the same day as the attacks on the

Jay-Z is photographed in a police car on April 13, 2001, after he was arrested for having a loaded handgun in his car. The handgun belonged to Jay-Z's bodyguard, and the charges of criminal possession of a gun were later dropped.

World Trade Center and the Pentagon. Despite this unfortunate timing, the album debuted at number one on the charts and went on to sell more than 450,000 copies in just its first week of release.

The Blueprint was critically praised by both fans and critics, many calling it his finest album ever. This was truly a Jay-Z album; nearly every song featured him alone, rapping lyrics less violent, yet more complex than any he'd ever done before. As Neil Strauss put it in *Rolling Stone*:

> This is how the rap game works: when someone is pushed, they push back harder. There's something about being persecuted, or at least believing oneself to be persecuted, that makes people embrace and reaffirm their own identity—witness Jay-Z's sixth album, *The Blueprint*.... Jay-Z was awaiting two criminal trials, one for gun possession, another for assault. In addition, he had become one of hip-hop's most dissed artists—with Nas, Prodigy of Mobb Deep, Jadakiss and others attacking him in song. Not unlike Tupac and his Makaveli persona, personal and legal problems have provoked Jay-Z to write what may his most personal, straightforward album. ...
>
> It's no longer enough to be the godfather he portrayed on *Reasonable Doubt*: he must now be God himself. Jay-Z makes earlier rap megalomaniacs pale in comparison as he identified with Jehova (nicknaming himself J-Hova, H.O.V.A., and, on this album's hits, Hovito and H-to-the-izzoh V-to-the-izzay). Elsewhere, he's the "God MC," "the eighth wonder of the world,".... Half of *The Blueprint* becomes, then, a battle album, in which Hova, from on high, attacks Nas, Prodigy, and all manner of prosecutors and persecutors. For much of the rest, Jay-Z gets real. ...
>
> In many ways, *The Blueprint* is a new-school old-school album, full of playground boasts, harmless battling and simple odes to the good life. Delving further into his roots, Jay-Z deepens his sound on *The Blueprint*. Here Jay-Z and his producers (especially Kanye West) turn to vintage soul, fueling almost every song with a stirring vocal sample. ... Jay-Z takes on most of the tracks single-handedly, without guest rappers. These tactics are ... the album's strength. He's a sharp, detailed writer, a meticulous craftsman and an influential stylist. ...

Other critics agreed, with *Vibe* magazine naming it the "Best Album of the Year." It even received a 5-mic (out of 5) rating from *The Source*, a distinction reserved for hip-hop classics. As AllMusic.com put it, the album is "a fully realized masterpiece."

Not only is the album a classic, but it has had a huge influence on hip-hop. The album's success helped to establish Kanye West as one of hip-hop's most celebrated producers and led the way to his own solo career, with such acclaimed albums as *The College Dropout* and *Late Registration*.

In addition, *The Blueprint* signaled a major stylistic shift in hip-hop production toward a more old-school soul/R & B and sample-reliant sound, replacing the keyboard-driven sound that had ruled for years. In many ways, it is one of the most influential albums of the first decade of the twenty-first century.

Jay-Z knew what he'd accomplished, as he said in an interview quoted in *Jay-Z . . . and the Roc-A-Fella Dynasty*:

> (This album is) definitely up there (as far as being one of my best), but I feel that all the time, so it ain't for me to say. It's for the people to say. . . . In rap everything moves so fast. You can be on top of your game and next year you're not. I just want to let them know I'm still right there on top.

With *The Blueprint*, Jay-Z did just that.

FEUDS

In the song "Takeover," Jay-Z took aim at his fellow rappers Nas and Prodigy of Mobb Deep, claiming that Prodigy had studied ballet and that Nas had lied about his street life before becoming a rapper, saying "you ain't live it / you witnessed it from your folks pad / You scribbled in your notebook and created your life." By attacking their street cred, he laid his own claim to be the only true "King of New York."

HOMOPHOBIA IN RAP

From its beginnings, hip-hop has often been criticized for being homophobic, meaning that its lyrics demonstrate an intense dislike and fear of gay people. One of the basic elements of hip-hop has been that of MCs battling one another in a war of words, always searching for the most degrading line or verse that one can say about an opponent. And in those battles, calling an opponent gay (or any of the often-used derogatory terms for gay) to attack his masculinity is one of the most used weapons in a rapper's arsenal. (Nas's attack on Jay-Z is a good example of this.)

But, as James Peterson, media coordinator for the Harvard University–sponsored Hip-Hop Archive Project, points out, "Some of that is homophobia, but because it's such a masculine culture, gay terminology is used to denote any kind of negative." However, even if such terms are not necessarily meant as homophobic, the words themselves are being used as weapons, meant to hurt, and serving to reinforce negative stereotypes of gay men.

Some rappers, like Kanye West, have had enough. In an interview for an MTV special, he became one of the first hip-hop artists to challenge the extreme negative stereotyping. Admitting that he had grown up homophobic, he changed his mind when he learned that one of his cousins was gay. "It was like a turning point when I was like, 'Yo, this is my cousin. I love him and I've been discriminating against gays.'"

He went on to say that hip-hop was always about "speaking your mind and about breaking down barriers, but everyone in hip-hop discriminates against gay people," adding that in slang, "gay" is "the opposite, the exact opposite word of hip-hop."

Kanye West has a message to everyone: "Not just hip-hop, but America just discriminates. And I just wanna . . . come on TV and tell my rappers, just tell my friends, 'Yo, stop it.' "

Jay-Z explained his reasons for the insults in an interview quoted in *Jay-Z . . . and the Roc-A-Fella Dynasty*:

> . . . for me it was like a sport. "Takeover" was like a sport. . . . I respected the dude lyrically. I feel like I'm on top of my game. I don't feel you can compare his [Nas] career to my career, but that's just my opinion. It just pushes everybody to sharpen their skills. That's what rap is about. It's a competitive sport. . . . Rappers don't really like each other, they never did. It's just so competitive. . . . Rap is a competitive sport. That's how it was built. . . .

It takes two people to feud. Nas responded to the insults in his song "Ether." In it he attacks Jay-Z for comparing himself to Notorious B.I.G., saying "First, Biggie's ya man, then you got the nerve to say you're better than Big . . . whyn't you let the late, great veteran live." Even more, throughout the song, Nas insults Jay-Z's masculinity (perhaps the worst insult that one rapper can give to another within the hip-hop community), hinting that Jay-Z is gay. And with that, the feud was on.

For the next two years, the two rappers traded insults in concerts, recordings, and interviews. Responding to "Ether," Jay-Z released the freestyle "Super Ugly," in which he boasted of having had an affair with the mother of Nas's child. With that, many felt that Jay-Z had gone too far.

It was Jay-Z's own mother who made him end the war of words. As he said in *Jay-Z . . . and the Roc-A-Fella Dynasty*:

> (In the end, my) mom put in a call and said, "That went too far." And she's never, ever called me about music. So I was like, "Okay, okay, okay. I'll go shut it down. I apologize." I felt like I didn't think about women's feeling or (Nas' former girlfriend's) feelings or even my mom. . . . I said some real mean things about Nas and his family and felt I was a

On his 2001 album, *The Blueprint*, Jay-Z recorded the song "Takeover" in which he attacks fellow rapper Nas *(above)*, triggering a rap feud that lasted many years. In the song, Jay insinuates that Nas doesn't have any street credibility. The insults and attacks continued until the two ended the conflict and performed together in a 2005 concert.

man about that by pulling the record publicly, although that wasn't a "gangster" thing to do. . . .

The war between Nas and Jay-Z slowly faded over the years, ending with a surprise joint concert in 2005. But before that happened, there were more albums, a retirement, and a world-famous girlfriend.

Going Out on Top

Jay-Z's next solo album, *The Blueprint 2: The Gift and the Curse*, released on November 12, 2002, continued his track record of releasing at least one album per year. The double album contained two hit singles: "Excuse Me Miss" and " '03 Bonnie and Clyde" featuring Jay-Z's girlfriend, Beyoncé Knowles, who was then a member of the hit group Destiny's Child.

The album, which sold more than 4 million copies in the United States alone, did not quite reach the level of critical acclaim as *The Blueprint*. Many critics felt that there weren't quite enough good songs on the album to warrant the length of a double album. (As if realizing this himself, Jay-Z released a single-disc version, *The Blueprint 2.1*, just five months later, containing half of the tracks from the original.)

Still, critics found much to praise on both versions of the album, with *Rolling Stone* calling it " . . . one more strong record from hip-hop's most dependable voice." AllMusic.com called Jay-Z " . . . the most respected rapper in the business," adding, "though his raps can't compete with the concentrated burst of *The Blueprint*, there's at least as many great tracks on tap, if only listeners have enough time to find them."

BUSINESS IS BOOMING

At this stage of his career, Jay-Z was so popular that he was constantly being offered endorsements from major corporations. One of them, Reebok, reached an agreement with him to introduce the S. Carter shoe collection, which made Jay-Z the first nonathlete to have an athletic shoe named after him. As an indicator of the power of his name, in just its first week of availability, the shoes had sold out everywhere, and pairs were being sold on eBay for double their suggested retail price.

Rocawear was also doing well, its value in 2003 estimated at over $300 million. With its line expanded to include both women's and children's clothing, it had become a clothing line for the entire family.

Always looking to expand his business empire, Jay-Z, as co-owner, opened New York City's 40/40 Club, an upscale sports bar, in 2003. Two years later, a second club opened in Atlantic City, and there are plans to open additional clubs in Los Angeles and Singapore. Roc-A-Fella also distributes Armandale, a Scottish vodka, in the United States.

And, perhaps most excitingly for Jay-Z on a personal level, in 2004 he became part-owner of the New Jersey Nets NBA team, paying a reported $4.5 million. Regarding this, he told *Rolling Stone*, "I was happy to cut that check!"

He told *Entertainment Weekly* just how much purchasing the team meant to him. "For a kid growing up in the Marcy Projects to be involved with [owning] a professional basketball team is way beyond anyone's dream. You may think you can

Jay-Z signs autographs at the release of his signature footwear collection, the S. Carter Collection by Reebok in 2003. Jay-Z was the first nonathlete to get a signature shoe from the company. After the shoe was unveiled on November 21, 2003, it became the fastest selling shoe in Reebok history.

Jay-Z is co-owner of the popular, upscale 40/40 nightclub. The club opened in Manhattan and, due to its growing success, a second club has opened in Atlantic City. There are plans for additional clubs in Los Angeles and Singapore. In the photograph above, Jay-Z *(left)* poses with basketball great Magic Johnson at the launch party for the 40/40 club in Atlantic City.

make it to [play in] the NBA, and that's a lofty dream. You never have the dream that you're gonna own the team. Every time I sit there and look around the table, I'm like, Wow, this is real, I'm on the board."

The Nets' new owners hope to move the team from New Jersey to a new arena in Brooklyn, to be called Barclays Center.

One can imagine that Jay-Z is thrilled to be part of the team that will bring professional basketball—as well as jobs, money, and a sense of pride—to his hometown.

Indeed, his newly amassed wealth brought an increased sense of responsibility to give back to the community. For years, he has been involved in a number of philanthropic efforts, including supporting the New York Mission Society, and organizing and funding his annual Jay-Z Santa Claus Toy Drive. In this role, remembering what it was like to be poor during Christmas, he brings toys to needy kids at Marcy Projects.

He has also contributed to numerous charities related to the September 11 attacks, performed at countless benefits concerts, and donated the entire proceeds of his November 2003 retirement concert to charity.

PERSONAL LIFE

Part of the mystique of Jay-Z is that he keeps his private life private. He talks about his music, his life before rap, but never about his personal relationships. It is widely known, however, that he and Beyoncé Knowles have had a long-term relationship, probably dating back to 1999.

Since then, they have appeared in public together, supplied vocals on each other's albums (Jay-Z on Beyoncé's smash hits "Crazy in Love" and "Déjà Vu," and Beyoncé on Jay-Z's "'03 Bonnie and Clyde" and "Hollywood"), and performed in concert together. What neither of them will do, however, is talk publicly about the relationship. As Jay-Z said in an interview quoted in *Jay-Z . . . and the Roc-A-Fella Dynasty*, "We don't play with our relationship. . . . In celebrity relationships, the only news is when people get together and when they break up. . . . We try not to do anything to heighten anybody's interest. . . ."

Though his relationship with Beyoncé was going strong, the year 2004 saw both the beginning and end of a newfound relationship with his father. After a nearly 20-year separation, it was Jay-Z's mother, Gloria, who urged the reconciliation. She told Jay-Z that his father, Adnis, was dying. She informed him that even though he had become enormously successful, there would be a huge part missing from his life until he'd come to terms with his father.

Not surprisingly, their reunion was strained at the beginning. What can someone say to a father he hasn't seen or heard from for so long? (Jay-Z, though, was struck by the physical similarities between the two: "It was like looking in a mirror," he says in *Jay-Z . . . and the Roc-A-Fella Records Dynasty*.) But after a relatively short period of time, the two began to talk, and his father apologized. Jay-Z described the scene: "He finally broke down and admitted he was wrong. He said he was sorry. Really sorry . . . I told him everything that was on my mind. And we shook hands, like men . . . I'm sure that was something he'd wanted to say to me for years."

Within just a few months of their meeting, Jay-Z's father died. Jay-Z, while sorry for this loss, was glad that he and his father had been able to come together before his father's passing. He said, "I was able to tell [my father] how I felt and put those negative feelings to rest. . . . The only way that I can be open completely even now is because of [the] timing [of it all]. Because I buried my father with [that] understanding between us."

At the same time, disagreements were growing between Jay-Z and his copartners at Roc-A-Fella, Damon Dash and Kareem "Biggs" Burke. They were unable to reach an understanding regarding the direction that the various companies owned by Roc-A-Fella should take, and their differing management styles would not allow them to reach a common ground.

Ultimately, the partners agreed to sell the label to Def Jam. Dash currently operates the recently founded Damon Dash Music Group as a joint venture with Island Def Jam, producing such former Roc-A-Fella artists as Beanie Sigel.

Although Jay-Z is in a high-profile romance with singer and actress Beyoncé Knowles, the two never speak of their relationship in public. But the two music stars perform together quite often, dueting on songs such as "Bonnie and Clyde," "Crazy in Love," and "Déjà vu." Photographed above, Jay-Z and Beyoncé perform "Crazy in Love" at the 2003 BET Awards.

JAY-Z AND R. KELLY

While this was going on, Jay-Z was dealing with problems dating back to a 2002 album on which he had collaborated with R & B singer R. Kelly entitled *The Best of Both Worlds*. Around the time the album was released, stories of a sex tape and related sexual scandals involving R. Kelly dominated the news. Because of the unfavorable publicity, sales of the album were disappointing, and Jay-Z withdrew from plans for a national tour after R. Kelly was accused of both statutory rape and assault.

In August 2004, eager to tie up any loose ends in his life as a performer, Jay-Z decided to reunite with R. Kelly and record a new album, *Unfinished Business*, and finally begin the Best of Both Worlds tour. The tour was scheduled to perform in 40 cities, and sold-out crowds were expected. But, as happened two years earlier, the tour soon fell apart.

Different opinions arose as to why the tour collapsed. Some say that Jay-Z was jealous of the audience affection for R. Kelly. Others argue that money issues are what derailed the tour. A majority of people, including Jay-Z, claim that it was R. Kelly's behavior that caused the tour to fail.

Several shows had to be canceled, and on one date, R. Kelly skipped the show, appearing instead at a McDonald's drive-in serving fans. On October 29, while appearing at Madison Square Garden, Kelly left the stage, claiming that he'd seen a gun in the audience, even though the Garden had a 20-year record of no weapon discovery or audience violence.

The crowd was searched, but no weapons were discovered. Meanwhile, Kelly also claimed that he and some of his staff had been sprayed backstage with pepper spray by a member of Jay-Z's entourage. The two were unable to work together after that, but Jay-Z continued the tour, along with help by special guest performers such as Usher, Mary J. Blige, and Snoop Dog.

In 2004, Jay-Z and R. Kelly embarked on a 40-city, sold-out tour called The Best of Both Worlds. The tour quickly fell apart due to conflicts between the two artists. R. Kelly left the tour, and Jay-Z continued to perform with special guest stars such as Mary J. Blige and Snoop Dog. Pictured above, Jay-Z *(left)* and R. Kelly perform together on the first stop of their tour.

RETIREMENT

Fortunately for Jay-Z, the problems with his business and the R. Kelly tour were minor compared with the success of what was billed as his final album, *The Black Album*, released in November of 2003.

Going into the studio to record the album, Jay-Z knew exactly what he wanted to do. As he said in an interview quoted in *Jay-Z . . . and the Roc-A-Fella Dynasty,* "[I]t's my last album. I want it to be the prequel to *Reasonable Doubt.* I want my mother to open it, then I go through my life. . . . Then it ends." The album was a celebration of Jay-Z's legacy as a recording artist. *Vibe* had this to say about the album:

> " . . . they say they never really miss you 'til you are dead or you gone," Jay-Z raps on the visceral "December 4th" (named for his birthdate). And with that, the first lyrics on his final album are earborne.

AllMusic.com added to the chorus of praise:

> If *The Black Album* is Jay-Z's last, as he publicly stated it will be, it illustrates an artist going out in top form. For years Shawn Carter has been the best rapper *and* the most popular, a man who can strut the player lifestyle with one track and become the eloquent hip-hop everyman with the next. . . . The . . . track "What More Can I Say," offers proof that he's one of the best of all time, and a look into what made him that way: "God forgive me for my brash delivery/but I remember vividly what these streets did to me." . . . The only issue that's puzzling about *The Black Album* is why one of the best rappers needs to say goodbye—unless, of course, he's simply afraid of being taken for granted and wants listeners to imagine a rap world without him.

The Black Album deservedly was a huge success: It debuted at number one on the charts, sold more than 3 million copies in the United States to date, and spawned several singles, including the smash hit "99 Problems." It was quite a way to "end" a recording career—at the top.

BEYONCÉ KNOWLES

Role model and superstar, Beyoncé Giselle Knowles (born September 4, 1981), is an R & B singer, songwriter, record producer, actress, fashion designer, and model. She shot to fame as the creative force and lead singer of R & B girl group Destiny's Child, the world's best-selling female group of all time.

After a string of commercially successful and critically acclaimed releases with the group, Beyoncé released her solo debut album *Dangerously in Love* in 2003. That album became one of the biggest commercial successes of the year, topping the album charts in the United States and the United Kingdom. It spawned the smash hit singles "Crazy in Love" and "Baby Boy," and earned Knowles five Grammy Awards in a single night in 2004. Her second solo album, *B-Day*, has been equally as successful.

In recent years, she has also become a film star, appearing in such films as *Austin Powers in Goldmember*, *The Fighting Temptations*, and *The Pink Panther*. The musical film *Dreamgirls*, was a huge critical and commercial success, earning her two Golden Globe nominations: Best Actress, Motion Picture Musical or Comedy, and Best Original Song for "Listen." Only in her twenties, Beyoncé seems likely to maintain her esteemed career as long as she desires.

STEPPING AWAY FROM THE MIC

With a hugely successful retirement album and concert, Jay's retirement became official at the end of December 2004. At the same time came the announcement that Jay-Z, Dash, and Biggs had sold their 50-percent share of Roc-A-Fella Records to Def Jam for a figure rumored to be $30 million. To the casual observer, it looked like Jay-Z was serious about leaving the recording business altogether. Little did they know that Jay-Z was about to embark on one of the more startling moves of his career.

CEO

It was up to Island Def Jam Music Group chairman L.A. Reid to make the announcement. Shawn Carter—aka Jay-Z—former drug dealer and superstar rapper, was going to be the next president of Def Jam Records. As Reid said in the press release announcing the appointment:

> . . . after 10 years of successfully running Roc-A-Fella, Shawn has proved himself to be an astute businessman, in addition to the brilliant artistic talent that the world sees and hears. . . . I can think of no one more relevant and credible in the hip-hop community to build upon Def Jam's fantastic legacy and move the company into its next groundbreaking era.

It was a historic moment. Never before had a top artist been given control of such a large record label.

But if it's obvious why Reid would want to hire Jay-Z, why would Jay-Z, who'd been talking about retirement, take on this new role? For starters, he is always looking for new challenges, for new territories to conquer. Second, Def Jam made him a great offer, including turning over to him full ownership of the masters of all his records after ten years, giving him total control of his recording legacy. And, finally, he did it to make a difference in the black community. As he discussed in an interview in *Jay-Z . . . and the Roc-A-Fella Records Dynasty*, it was part of his drive to

> . . . succeed and open doors for the next generation just like Russell Simmons opened up the doors for me as far as fashion and music. I don't have any secret obsession. . . . It's just so that I can open up doors like on the executive level. There's a need for that . . . another thing . . . [I] like to challenge myself. . . . I was doing so much, that I felt like I had to challenge myself in other areas, and there's also a void on black executive side, you know. They have like head of black music, which is great, and things like that, but you know, just wanted to take it to the next level. . . . I have inherited two of the most important brands in hip-hop, Def Jam and Roc-A-Fella. . . . I feel this is a giant step for me and the entire artistic community.

Jay-Z began his new career on January 1, 2005. He admitted in an interview with *Fortune* magazine that he hadn't really thought in detail about what his new position would entail, admitting that "I'd never had a real job." But many of the financial aspects of the position are handled by Def Jam's corporate parent (although Jay-Z does sign off on all checks and payments), and many of the day-to-day aspects of running a corporation are handled by seven division heads who work beneath him.

So what exactly does he do? His primary job is to sign new talent, help to develop talent, and assist artists in producing the best albums, videos, and concerts possible. And it is because of his experience and reputation as a hip-hop artist that he has the credibility to tell others what they need to do. As Semtex, a London-based DJ who is urban promotions/A&R manager for Def Jam, told *Fortune*:

> . . . you know how people say they want to be "Like Mike" [in basketball]? In our industry, they want to be like Jay. And

RUSSELL SIMMONS

Cofounder with Rick Rubin of the pioneering hip-hop label Def Jam; founder of another label, Russell Simmons Music Group; and creator of the clothing fashion line Phat Farm, Russell Simmons is truly one of the godfathers of hip-hop.

Recently, he's been in the news questioning the direction that hip-hop has taken and calling for the removal of what he says are three "sexist and racist" words from songs. Acknowledging that the public was growing more angry about these terms, he said that they should be viewed in the same way as "extreme curse words." He asked both broadcasters and record companies to recommend guidelines for lyrical and visual standards and called for a private meeting of influential music executive leaders to discuss the issue.

Arguing that the use of some words are derogatory and disrespectful to listeners, he noted that "Our discussions are about the corporate social responsibility of the industry to voluntarily show respect to African-Americans and other persons of color, African-American women and to all women in lyrics and images."

not just because he's the best lyricist, but because he's taken control of his career. He inspires artists to reach for that too. If Jay-Z says you have to go back in the studio and write new bars, you've got to write new bars. If Jay-Z says your stage show isn't hot, it's not hot. You can't argue with him; he's sold millions of records.

His first year as president got off to a rocky start, with disappointing sales for new records by Memphis Bleek, Young Gunz, and Rihanna. Uncertain whether he'd made the right decision, Jay-Z told *Rolling Stone*, "I wanted to quit right away. There was nothing fresh, no excitement. . . . I said, 'Where's the passion.'"

But then it dawned on him that it was exactly his job to inject the passion. And now he feels comfortable in his position. He's started two labels, Roc La Familia and Def Jam Left, signed a mix of new and experienced artists, and feels confident about the future. Sitting in his office, described by *Rolling Stone* as having "great views across the Hudson River, a big chocolate-brown couch, a huge-screen TV bookended by gigantic speakers and, next to his desk, a large monitor for his e-mails," he looks and acts every inch the CEO.

"I DECLARE WAR"

Although Jay-Z was fully involved in his role as president of Def Jam, he still wasn't completely willing to give up performing. On October 27, 2005, Jay-Z headlined New York FM radio's Power 105.1 annual concert, Powerhouse. The show was entitled the "I Declare War" concert, which led to intense speculation in the weeks before the event as to whom exactly Jay-Z would declare war on. Given his history of "declaring war" on other rappers who had taken lyrical shots at him, many believed that the concert would give him the stage to declare an all-out "war" on his rivals.

The theme of the concert was Jay-Z's position as president and CEO of Def Jam, and the stage became a mock version of

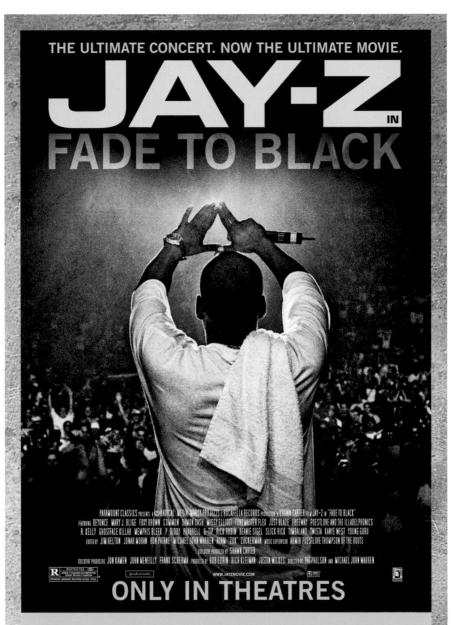

Jay-Z's 2004 documentary *Fade to Black* chronicles his sold-out performance at Madison Square Garden. The concert was to be his final show, as he announced his retirement that same year. The film documented the spectacular night that culminated all of Jay-Z's hard work as a performer and lyricist.

Jay-Z performs at the 2005 "I Declare War" concert *(above)*. The show opened with Jay-Z sitting in a mock-up of the Oval Office, surrounded by "Secret Service agents." It was during this concert that Jay-Z ended his longstanding feud with Nas.

the White House's Oval Office. Many artists from the old roster of Roc-A-Fella Records made appearances, as well as Ne-Yo, Teairra Mari, T.I., Young Jeezy, Akon, Kanye West, Paul Wall, the LOX, and P. Diddy.

At the end of the concert, Jay-Z had a surprise for hip-hop fans expecting the start of a new feud between rappers. Instead of declaring war, Jay-Z declared that he was the "United Nations of this rap $#?%" and officially ended the long-standing riff between Nas and him. In a brilliant piece of stagecraft, Nas made a surprise appearance; the two rivals shook hands and then shared the stage together to perform Jay-Z's "Dead Presidents" blended with Nas's song "The World Is Yours," from which "Dead Presidents" had sampled the chorus vocals.

Other feuds also came to an end at the Powerhouse show. The event brought P. Diddy and the LOX together for the first time in years—the pair had had a longstanding animosity due to contract disputes. Shortly after the concert, the two agreed to end their feud.

As the year 2005 came to an end, Jay sat down with *Rolling Stone* to discuss his career and life as CEO. At the end of the interview, he was asked the question on everybody's mind: "How close are you to making a record?" He replied that he wasn't close, that he didn't have "the itch" to make a record, but added that he still kept writing songs in his head: "I've got six or seven good ones and a bunch of other silly ideas." He builds on and remembers these songs by rhyming when he showers: "Every day, every shower."

The question, then, was left unanswered: When would Jay-Z come out of retirement and reclaim his throne?

The Return

By spring 2006, the news had hit the streets: Jay-Z was returning to record another album. As he said in an interview with *Entertainment Weekly,* "It was the worst retirement, maybe, in history."

As satisfying as running Def Jam was, it's clear that it didn't completely satisfy all of Jay-Z's professional needs. But, as he pointed out to *Entertainment Weekly,* it wasn't any one thing that brought him back to the recording studio. "It wasn't like a defining moment. Something, when you love it, is always tugging at you and itching at you, and I was putting it off and putting it off. I started fumbling around to see if it felt good."

Obviously it did. Working with an all-star group of producers, including Dr. Dre, Kanye West, the Neptunes, and Chris Martin of Coldplay, and guest artists John Legend, Usher,

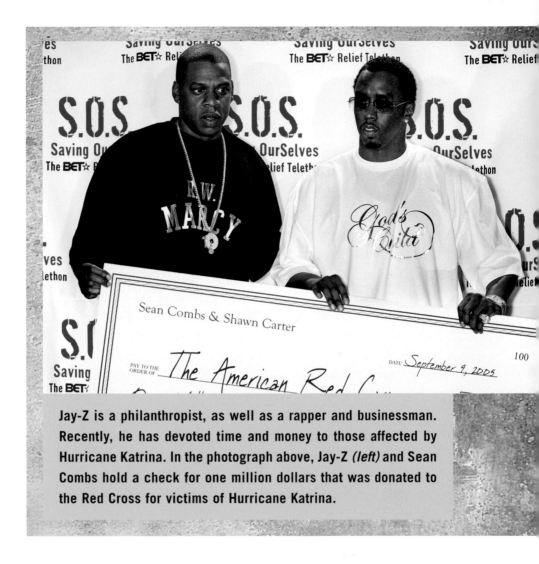

Jay-Z is a philanthropist, as well as a rapper and businessman. Recently, he has devoted time and money to those affected by Hurricane Katrina. In the photograph above, Jay-Z *(left)* and Sean Combs hold a check for one million dollars that was donated to the Red Cross for victims of Hurricane Katrina.

Pharrell Williams, Beyoncé, Ne-Yo and Chris Martin, the album was released on November 21, 2006. Entitled *Kingdom Come*, the name came from the DC Comics limited series of the same name, where Superman returns from self-exile to an apocalyptic and chaotic world. Continuing Jay-Z's winning streak, the album debuted at number one, selling more than 680,000 copies in its first week, the best first-week sales of his career. Clearly, the two-year absence had done nothing to diminish his appeal.

(continues on page 98)

THE GREY ALBUM

Interestingly, one of Jay-Z's best-known and most critically acclaimed albums is one that he didn't record himself. It's known as *The Grey Album*.

The Grey Album is an album by Danger Mouse that uses an a cappella version of *The Black Album* (Jay-Z's raps without any of the original instrumental backing) and combines it with instrumentals assembled from a number of unauthorized samples from the classic album *The Beatles* (commonly known as *The White Album*).

While Danger Mouse had no legal permission to use the samples from *The White Album*, the a cappella version of *The Black Album* had been released for the implicit purpose of encouraging mashups and remixes. EMI, the copyright owner of the Beatles' material, ordered Danger Mouse and retailers to cease distribution of the album. In protest, on February 24, 2004, many Web sites posted copies of *The Grey Album* for free download on their sites for 24 hours. The protest made *The Grey Album* the number-one album in the United States on that date, with more than 100,000 copies being downloaded on that day alone.

The album became extraordinarily popular due in no small part to the controversy and publicity. It received widespread critical acclaim as well, even being named to the Best of 2004 by *Entertainment Weekly* magazine.

The Grey Album is only one of several remixes of *The Black Album*, spurred by Jay-Z's release of the a cappellas. Other artists "mashed up" with Jay-Z include Weezer, Pavement, Prince, Metallica, and Wu-Tang Clan.

In 2006, Jay-Z came out of retirement and released his come-back album, *Kingdom Come*. The album featured the hit single "Show Me What You Got," and has sold more than 2 million copies. Jay-Z continues to succeed in all of his many business and artistic ventures.

(continued from page 95)

SITTING ON TOP OF THE WORLD

In a recording career spanning just over a decade, Jay-Z has come a long way from life at Marcy Projects. With a personal worth estimated at over $340 million, he lives a life that few ever achieve. His deal with Universal (the parent company of Def Jam Records) pays him between $8 million and $10 million a year. He's president of Roc-A-Fella Records. He is the owner of two multimillion-dollar apartments, one of them a 10,000-square-foot loft in Tribeca worth an estimated $7.5 million and the other a penthouse at the Time Warner Center near Central Park worth more than $10 million. (From this penthouse, he can see the penthouse owned by his girlfriend, Beyoncé.)

But more than the financial rewards, Jay-Z owns an artistic and personal legacy worthy of admiration. As a rapper, he has recorded classic albums that have changed the face of hip-hop and led to him being called by MTV "the greatest MC of all time." As a philanthropist, he has continued to give back, donating a million dollars to the Hurricane Katrina cause and addressing the global water crisis in Turkey and South Africa.

And as a man, he has demonstrated the possibility of overcoming adversity, turning one's back on the lure of easy money, and following one's dream. He's a man proud of where he came from, of what he's achieved, and what he still hopes to accomplish. As he said in an interview quoted in *Jay-Z . . . and the Roc-A-Fella Dynasty,*

> Here I am, a guy from Marcy Projects making people react
> to the music I create in my head. . . . Most of the time, I walk
> around feeling real blessed. If God had shown me this life
> beforehand, complete with all the drama, I'd say—without
> pause—I'll take it.

DISCOGRAPHY

1996   *Reasonable Doubt*
1997   *In My Lifetime, Vol. 1*
1998   *Vol. 2: Hard Knock Life*
1999   *Vol. 3: Life and Times of S. Carter*
2000   *The Dynasty: Roc La Familia*
2001   *The Blueprint*
       Jay-Z: Unplugged
2002   *The Best of Both Worlds* (with R. Kelly)
       The Blueprint 2: The Gift and the Curse
2003   *The Blueprint 2.1*
       The Black Album
2004   *Unfinished Business* (with R. Kelly)
       Collision Course (with Linkin Park)
2006   *Kingdom Come*

FILMOGRAPHY

1998   *Streets Is Watching*
2000   *Hard Knock Life*
2002   *State Property*
2002   *Paper Soldiers*
2004   *Fade to Black*
2006   *Diary of Jay-Z: Water for Life* (http://www.waterforlife
       .mtv.com)

1969 Shawn Corey Carter, better known as Jay-Z, is born on December 4 to Gloria Carter and Adnis Reeves in Brooklyn, New York.

1982 Adnis Reeves leaves the Carter home, an act that strains the entire family and contributes to Shawn's decision to leave school and turn to the streets.

1988–1994 Jay-Z begins to appreciate his talent as a rapper. Records "Hawaiian Sophie" with Jaz-O, who becomes a mentor for him. Appears on a few other records, but, lacking a recording contract, continues to sell drugs.

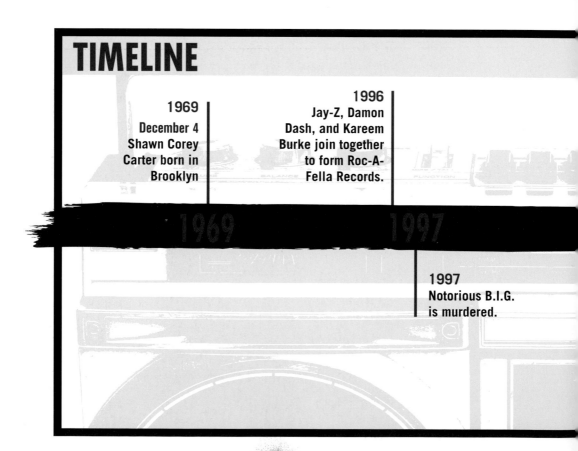

TIMELINE

1969

December 4
Shawn Corey
Carter born in
Brooklyn

1996
Jay-Z, Damon
Dash, and Kareem
Burke join together
to form Roc-A-
Fella Records.

1969

1997

1997
Notorious B.I.G.
is murdered.

1995   Meets aspiring entrepreneur Damon Dash, who signs him to a management deal.

1996   Jay-Z, Dash, and Kareem Burke join together to form Roc-A-Fella Records. Jay-Z's debut album, *Reasonable Doubt*, is released and is soon recognized as a hip-hop classic. Roc-A-Fella begins negotiations with Def Jam Records.

1997   Jay-Z's friend Notorious B.I.G. is murdered in Los Angeles. Def Jam and Roc-A-Fella come to a business agreement, and *In My Lifetime, Vol. 1* is released. The album is a commercial success.

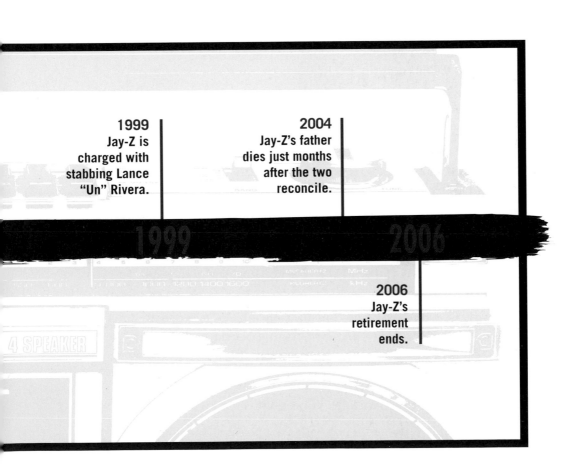

1999
Jay-Z is
charged with
stabbing Lance
"Un" Rivera.

2004
Jay-Z's father
dies just months
after the two
reconcile.

2006
Jay-Z's
retirement
ends.

1998   *Vol. 2: Hard Knock Life* is released, becoming Jay-Z's biggest hit to date, supported by a 52-city tour. The Rocawear clothing line is introduced.

1999   Release of *Vol.3: Life and Times of S. Carter* to both critical and popular acclaim. In December, Jay-Z is in attendance at a New York City nightclub when Lance "Un" Rivera is stabbed. He is charged with the stabbing but declares his innocence.

2000   *The Dynasty: Roc La Familia*, an album designed to promote Roc-A-Fella recording artists, is released. Jay-Z accepts a plea agreement rather than standing trial for Un's stabbing.

2001   Jay-Z releases *The Blueprint* on September 11, the same date as the terrorist attacks on the World Trade Center and the Pentagon. It receives huge sales and near unanimous critical acclaim.

2002   His first double album, *The Blueprint 2*, is released. Several months later, a single-disc version is released.

2003   *The Black Album*, Jay-Z's "retirement album," is released. Jay-Z and friends perform his "farewell concert" at Madison Square Garden.

2004   Adnis Reeves dies, just months after reconciling with his son. Jay-Z begins negotiations with both Warner Music Group and Def Jam Records before signing with Def Jam Recording as president and CEO. Begins tour with R. Kelly, but the tour quickly falls apart. R. Kelly leaves, and Jay-Z completes the tour with the assistance of other special guests.

2005   On January 1, Jay-Z begins his new career with Def Jam. "I Declare War" concert ends feud with Nas.

2006   The retirement ends with the release of *Kingdom Come* on November 1.

GLOSSARY

a capella   Vocals sung without musical accompaniment.

cross-marketing   A business practice in which one event or product is used to promote or advertise another. For example, Roc-A-Fella would use a concert appearance or video by Jay-Z to promote both his music and his Rocawear clothing, both of which were owned by Roc-A-Fella.

flow   The ability to start and then maintain a verse of lyrics.

freestyle rap   An improvisational form of rapping, performed with few or no previously composed lyrics. It is nonscripted, nonrehearsed, uncut, and the rawest form of hip-hop. Freestyle rapping forces the rapper to think quickly on the spot, describe his or her surroundings, and rap without too much thought put into it.

lick   An improvised musical phrase.

mashup   A musical form that consists of the combination (usually by digital means) of the instrumentation from one song with the vocals from another. Typically, the music and vocals belong to completely different genres of music.

master   An original recording from which copies can be made.

MC   Originally short for "master of ceremonies." In hip-hop, the MC puts down the rhymes over the back beats and music.

sample   A portion of a previously recorded piece of music that is then used, or "sampled," in a new piece of music. Sampling is an integral part of hip-hop music.

BIBLIOGRAPHY

Bankston, John. *Jay-Z.* Hockessin, DE: Mitchell Lane Publishers, 2004.

Barnes, Geoff. *Jay-Z.* Broomall, PA: Mason Crest Publishers, 2007.

Birchmeier, Jason, "The Blueprint," Allmusic.com. Available online. http://www.allmusic.com/cg/amg.dll?p=amg&sql=10:309ss30qa3zg.

"The Blueprint, Vol. 2: The Gift and the Curse," Rollingstone.com. Available online. www.rollingstone.com/artists/jayz/albums/album255668review/5943959/the_blueprint_vol_2_the_gift_and_the_curse.

Brown, Jake. *Jay-Z . . . and the Roc-A-Fella Records Dynasty.* Phoenix, Ariz.: Colossus Books, 2005.

Bush, John. "The Black Album," Allmusic.com. Available online. http://www.allmusic.com/cg/amg.dll?p=amg&sql=10:is9ks39wa39g.

———. "The Blueprint 2: The Gift & the Curse," Allmusic.com. Available online. http://www.allmusic.com/cg/amg.dll?p=amg&sql=10:kz6gtr7tk15x.

———. "In My Lifetime, Vol. 1," Allmusic.com. Available online. http://www.allmusic.com/cg/amg.dll?p=amg&sql=10:uwaxqj4iojka.

"Call for End to Racist Rap Lyrics," BBC News. Available online. http://news.bbc.co.uk/2/hi/entertainment/6586787.stm.

Carmanica, Joe. "Biography of Jay-Z," RollingStone.com. Available online. http://www.rollingstone.com/artists/jayz/biography.

Collis, Clark. "Jay-Z Returns," EntertainmentWeekly.com. Available online. http://www.ew.com/ew/article/0,,1534551,00.html?print.

Ex, Kris. "Vol. 3, Life and Times of S. Carter," RollingStone .com. Available online. http://www.rollingstone.com/artists/ jayz/albums/album/209448/review.

Hira, Nadira. "America's Hippest CEO," CNNMoney.com. Available online. http://money.cnn.com/magazines/fortune/ fortune_archive/2005/10/17/8358069.

Huey, Steve. "Reasonable Doubt," Allmusic.com. Available online. http://www.allmusic.com/cg/amg.dll?p=amg&sql=10 :hzfpxqthldje~T1.

"Kanye West Calls for End to Gay Bashing," USAToday.com. Available online. http://www.usatoday.com/life/people/ 2005–08–18-kanye-west_x.htm.

"Rapper Common Shows That in Anti-Gay Genre, Lyrics May Change," Southern Voice. Available online. http://www.sova .com/2003/8–29/news/national/hiphop.cfm.

Roman, Julian. "Fade to Black: An Interview with Jay-Z," LatinoReview.com. Available online. http://www .latinoreview.com/films_2004/paramountclassics/ fadetoblack/jayz-interview.html.

Sheffield, Rob. "Kingdom Come," Rollingstone.com. Available online. http://www.rollingstone.com/reviews/album/ 12392104/review/12665411/kingdom_come.

Touré. "The Book of Jay." *Rolling Stone*, Issue 989 (December 15, 2005).

▶ ▸ FURTHER READING ■ ‖

BOOKS

Bogdanov, Vladimir, Chris Woodstra, Stephen Thomas Erlewine, John Bush, eds. *All Music Guide to Hip-Hop: The Definitive Guide to Rap and Hip-Hop.* San Francisco, Calif.: Backbeat Books, 2003.

Chang, Jeff. *Can't Stop, Won't Stop: A History of the Hip-Hop Generation.* New York: St. Martin's Press, 2005.

Coker, Cheo Hodari. *Unbelievable: The Life, Death, and Afterlife of the Notorious B.I.G.* New York: Three Rivers Press, 2004.

Gueraseva, Stacy. *Def Jam, Inc.: Russell Simmons, Rick Rubin, and the Extraordinary Story of the World's Most Influential Hip-Hop Label.* New York: One World/Ballantine, 2005.

Liles, Kevin, and Samantha Marshall. *Make It Happen: The Hip-Hop Generation Guide to Success.* New York: Atria, 2006.

WEB SITES

www.defjam.com

www.jayzfan.info

www.ohhla.com/YFA_jayz.html

www.rocafella.com

▶▶ PHOTO CREDITS ■ ▮▮

▶ ▶▶ INDEX ■ ‖

▶ ▶ ABOUT THE AUTHORS ■ ‖

DENNIS ABRAMS has written many biographies for young adults, including biographies of Anthony Horowitz, Hamid Karzai, Ty Cobb, Eminem, and the Beastie Boys. He attended Antioch College where he majored in English and communications. He currently lives in Houston, Texas.

CHUCK D redefined rap music and hip-hop culture as leader and co-founder of legendary rap group Public Enemy. His messages address weighty issues about race, rage and inequality with a jolting combination of intelligence and eloquence. A musician, writer, radio host, television guest, college lecturer, and activist, he is the creator of Rapstation.com, a multi-format home on the Web for the vast global hip-hop community.